RENEWALS 458-4574

DATE DUE

A Question of
Balance

A Question of Balance

Weighing the Options on
Global Warming Policies

William Nordhaus

Yale University Press   New Haven & London

Printed in the United States of America.

Library of Congress Control Number: 2007942915
ISBN: 978-0-300-13748-4

A catalogue record for this book is available from the British Library.

The paper in this book meets the guidelines for permanence and durability of the Committee on Production Guidelines for Book Longevity of the Council on Library Resources.

10 9 8 7 6 5 4 3 2 1

Simplicity is the highest form of sophistication.

—Leonardo

Contents

Acknowledgments

This research has received the generous support of Yale University, the National Science Foundation, the Department of Energy, and the Glaser Foundation. I am grateful to the program officers in those organizations who have provided critical support for this and early versions of the work for many foundation-years. An early version of Chapter 8 appeared in the *Review of Environmental Economics and Policy*, and a version of Chapter 9 appeared in the *Journal of Economic Literature*.

Skillful research assistance for the current effort has been provided by David Corderi, Steve Hao, Justin Lo, and Caroleen Verly. The author is grateful for comments on the many iterations of the model made by William Cline, Jae Edmonds, Roger Gordon, Arnulf Gruebler, Dale Jorgenson, Klaus Keller, Wolfgang Lutz, David Popp, John Reilly, Jeffrey Sachs, Robert Stavins, Richard Tol, Martin Weitzman, John Weyant, Zili Yang, and Gary Yohe, as well as many anonymous referees and reviewers. Particular thanks go to Zili Yang, who has collaborated on several rounds of the DICE-model design and is currently working on a joint project for the regional version, the RICE model.

In October 2007, the Nobel Peace Prize was awarded to the Intergovernmental Panel on Climate Change (IPCC) and Albert Gore Jr. "for their efforts to build up and disseminate greater knowledge about man-made climate change, and to lay the foundations for the measures that are needed to counteract such change." This award highlights the importance and complexity of the scientific, social, environmental, and policy issues involved in global warming. The present work is deeply indebted to the extraordinary contributions of social and natural scientists working in this area. The author has benefited from the fundamental research of an earlier generation of researchers, notably Tjalling Koopmans, Lester Machta, Alan Manne, Howard Raiffa, Roger Ravelle, Thomas Schelling, Joseph Smagorinsky, Robert Solow, and James Tobin, as well as dozens of friends and colleagues who have contributed to the four assessment reports of the IPCC. To paraphrase Newton, if I have seen anything, it is by standing on the shoulders of giants. Therefore, it is to the giants of the past and to the current generation of social and natural scientists working on global warming that this book is dedicated.

Introduction

The issues involved in understanding global warming and taking actions to slow its harmful impacts are the major environmental challenge of the modern age. Global warming poses a unique mix of problems that arise from the fact that global warming is a global public good, is likely to be costly to slow or prevent, has daunting scientific and economic uncertainties, and will cast a shadow over the globe for decades, perhaps even centuries, to come.

The challenge of coping with global warming is particularly difficult because it spans many disciplines and parts of society. Ecologists may see it as a threat to ecosystems, marine biologists as a problem leading to ocean acidification, utilities as a debit on their balance sheets, and coal miners as an existential threat to their livelihood. Businesses may view global warming as either an opportunity or a hazard, politicians as a great issue as long as they do not need to mention taxes, ski resorts as a mortal danger to their already-short seasons, golfers as a boon to year-round recreation, and poor countries as a threat to their farmers, as well as a source of financial and technological aid. This multifaceted nature also poses a challenge to natural and social scientists, who must incorporate a wide variety of geophysical, economic, and political disciplines into their diagnoses and prescriptions.

This is the age of global warming—and of global-warming studies. This book uses the tools of economics and mathematical modeling to analyze efficient and inefficient approaches to slowing global warming. It describes a small but comprehensive model of the economy and climate called the DICE-2007 model, for Dynamic Integrated model of Climate and the Economy.

This book reports on a completely revised version of earlier models developed by the author and collaborators to understand the economic and environmental dynamics of alternative approaches to slowing global warming. It represents the fifth major version of modeling efforts, with earlier versions developed in the periods 1974–1979, 1980–1982, 1990–1994, and 1997–2000.[1] Many of the equations and details have changed during the different generations, but the basic modeling philosophy remains unchanged: to incorporate the latest economic and scientific knowledge and to capture the major elements of the economics of climate change in as simple and transparent a fashion as possible. The guiding philosophy is, in Leonardo's words, that "simplicity is the highest form of sophistication."

The book combines a description of the new version of the DICE model with analyses of several major issues and policy proposals. We begin with a brief outline of the major chapters for those who would like a map of the terrain.

Chapter 1 is a "Summary for the Concerned Citizen" that describes the underlying approach and major results of the study. This chapter stands alone and can usefully be read by noneconomists who want a broad overview, as well as by specialists who would like an intuitive summary.

Chapter 2 provides a verbal description of the DICE model. Chapter 3 provides a detailed description of the model's equations. The actual equations of the model are presented in the Appendix.

Chapter 4 describes the alternative policies that are analyzed in the computer runs. These include everything from the current Kyoto Protocol to an idealized perfectly efficient or "optimal" economic approach. Chapter 5 presents the major analytical results of the different policies, including the economic impacts, the carbon prices and control rates, and the effects on greenhouse-gas concentrations and temperature.

Chapters 6 through 9 provide further analyses using the DICE model. Chapter 6 begins with an analysis of the impacts of incomplete participation. This new modeling approach is able to capture analytically the economic and geophysical impacts of policies that include only a fraction of countries or sectors; it shows the importance of full participation. Chapter 7 presents preliminary results on the impacts of uncertainty on policies and outcomes. Chapter 8 is a policy-oriented chapter that examines the two major approaches to controlling emissions—prices and quantities—and describes the surprising advantages of price-type approaches.

Chapter 9 provides an analysis, using the DICE-model framework, of the recent *Stern Review* of the economics of climate change. The final chapter contains some reservations about the results and then presents the major conclusions of the study. The GAMS computer code, the derivation of the model, and technical details are provided in "Accompanying Notes and Documentation on Development of DICE-2007 Model" (Nordhaus 2007a). The Web site for the DICE model and results is http://www.econ.yale.edu/~nordhaus/homepage/DICE2007.htm.

I

Summary for the Concerned Citizen

Often, technical studies of global warming begin with an executive summary for policymakers. Instead, I would like to provide a summary for the audience of concerned citizens. The points that follow are prepared for both scientists and nonspecialists who would like a succinct statement of what economics, or at least the economics in this book, concludes about the dilemmas posed by global warming.

Global warming has taken center stage in the international environmental arena during the past decade. Concerned and disinterested analysts across the entire spectrum of economic and scientific research take the prospects for a warmer world seriously. A careful look at the issues reveals that there is at present no obvious answer as to how fast nations should move to slow climate change. Neither extreme—either do nothing or stop global warming in its tracks—is a sensible course of action. Any well-designed policy must balance the economic costs of actions today with their corresponding future economic and ecological benefits. How to balance

costs and benefits is the central question addressed by
this book.

Overview of the Issue of Global Warming

The underlying premise of this book is that global warming
is a serious, perhaps even a grave, societal issue. The scientific
basis of global warming is well established. The core problem
is that the burning of fossil (or carbon-based) fuels such as
coal, oil, and natural gas leads to emissions of carbon dioxide
(CO_2).

Gases such as CO_2, methane, nitrous oxide, and halocar-
bons are called greenhouse gases (GHGs). They tend to accu-
mulate in the atmosphere and have a very long residence time,
from decades to centuries. Higher concentrations of GHGs
lead to surface warming of the land and oceans. These warming effects are indirectly amplified through feedback effects
in the atmosphere, oceans, and land. The resulting climate
changes, such as changes in temperature extremes, precipitation patterns, storm location and frequency, snowpacks, river
runoff and water availability, and ice sheets, may have profound impacts on biological and human activities that are sensitive to the climate.

Although the exact future pace and extent of warming are
highly uncertain—particularly beyond the next few decades—
there can be little scientific doubt that the world has embarked
on a major series of geophysical changes that are unprece-
dented in the past few thousand years. Scientists have detected
early symptoms of this syndrome clearly in several areas:
Emissions and atmospheric concentrations of greenhouse
gases are rising, there are signs of rapidly increasing average
surface temperatures, and scientists have detected diagnostic

signals—such as greater high-latitude warming—that are distinguishing indicators of this particular type of warming. Recent evidence and model predictions suggest that global mean surface temperature will rise sharply in the next century and beyond. *Climate Change 2007*, the Fourth Assessment Report of the Intergovernmental Panel on Climate Change (IPCC 2007a, 2007b), gives a best estimate of the global temperature increase over the coming century as from 1.8 to 4.0°C. Although this seems like a small change, it is much more rapid than any changes that have occurred in the past 10,000 years.

Global emissions of CO_2 in 2006 were estimated to be around 7.5 billion tons of carbon. It will be helpful to bring this astronomical number down to the level of the individual. Suppose that you drive 10,000 miles a year in a car that gets 28 miles per gallon. Your car will emit about 1 ton of carbon per year. (While this book focuses on carbon weight, other studies sometimes discuss emissions in terms of tons of CO_2, which has a weight 3.67 times the weight of carbon. In this case, your automobile emissions are about 4 tons of CO_2 per year.) Or you might consider a typical U.S. household, which uses about 10,000 kilowatt-hours (kWh) of electricity each year. If this electricity were generated from coal, it would release about 3 tons of carbon (or 11 tons of CO_2) per year. On the other hand, if the electricity were generated from nuclear power, or if you rode a bicycle to work, the carbon emissions of these activities would be close to zero. In all, the United States emits about 1.6 billion tons of carbon a year, which is slightly more than 5 tons per person annually. For the world, the emissions rate is about 1.25 tons per person.

The Economic Approach to
Climate-Change Policy

This book uses an economic approach to weighing alternative options for dealing with climate change. The essence of an economic analysis is to convert or translate all economic activities into a common unit of account and then to compare different approaches by their impact on the total amount. The units are generally the value of goods in constant prices (such as 2005 U.S. dollars). However, the values are not really money. Rather, they represent a standard bundle of goods and services (such as $1,000 worth of food, $3,000 of housing, $900 of medical services, and so forth). So we are really translating all activities into the number of such standardized bundles.

To illustrate the economic approach, suppose that an economy produces only corn. We might decide to reduce corn consumption today and store it for the future to offset the damages from climate change on future corn production. In weighing this policy, we consider the economic value of corn both today and in the future in order to decide how much corn to store and how much to consume today. In a complete economic account, "corn" would be all economic consumption. It would include all market goods and services, as well as the value of nonmarket and environmental goods and services. That is, economic welfare—properly measured—should include everything that is of value to people, even if those things are not included in the marketplace.

The central questions posed by economic approaches to climate change are the following: How sharply should countries reduce CO_2 and other GHG emissions? What should be the time profile of emissions reductions? How should the reductions be distributed across industries and countries? Other important and politically divisive issues concern how to impose cuts on consumers and businesses. Should there be a system of emissions limits imposed on firms, industries, and nations? Or should emissions reductions be imposed primarily through taxes on GHGs? What should be the relative contributions of rich and poor households or nations?

In practice, an economic analysis of climate change weighs the costs of slowing climate change against the damages of more rapid climate change. On the side of the costs of slowing climate change, countries must consider whether, and by how much, to reduce their GHG emissions. Reducing GHGs, particularly if the reductions are to be deep, will primarily require taking costly steps to reduce CO_2 emissions. Some steps involve reducing the use of fossil fuels; others involve using different production techniques or alternative fuels and energy sources. Societies have considerable experience in employing different approaches to changing energy production and use patterns. Economic history and analysis indicate that it will be most effective to use the market mechanism, primarily higher prices on carbon fuels, to give signals and provide incentives for consumers and firms to change their energy use and reduce their carbon emissions. In the longer run, higher carbon prices will provide incentives for firms to develop new technologies to ease the transition to a low-carbon future.

On the side of climate damages, our knowledge is very meager. For most of the time span of human civilizations, global climatic patterns have stayed within a very narrow range, varying at most a few tenths of a degree Celsius (°C) from century to century. Human settlements, along with their ecosystems and pests, have generally adapted to the climates and geophysical features they have grown up with. Economic studies suggest that those parts of the economy that are insulated from climate, such as air-conditioned houses and most manufacturing operations, will be little affected directly by climatic change during the next century or so.

However, those human and natural systems that are "unmanaged," such as rain-fed agriculture, seasonal snow-packs and river runoffs, and most natural ecosystems, may be significantly affected. Although economic studies in this area are subject to large uncertainties, the best guess in this book is that the economic damages from climate change with no interventions will be on the order of 2.5 percent of world output per year by the end of the twenty-first century. The damages are likely to be most heavily concentrated in low-income and tropical regions such as tropical Africa and India. Although some countries may benefit from climate change, there is likely to be significant disruption in any area that is closely tied to climate-sensitive physical systems, whether through rivers, ports, hurricanes, monsoons, permafrost, pests, diseases, frosts, or droughts.

The DICE Model of the Economics of Climate Change

The purpose of this book is to examine the economics of climate change in the framework of the DICE model, which is an acronym for Dynamic Integrated model of Climate and the Economy. The DICE model is the latest generation in a series of models in this area. The model links the factors affecting economic growth, CO_2 emissions, the carbon cycle, climate change, climatic damages, and climate-change policies. The equations of the model are taken from different disciplines—

economics, ecology, and the earth sciences. They are then run using mathematical optimization software so that the economic and environmental outcomes can be projected.

The DICE model views the economics of climate change from the perspective of economic growth theory. In this approach, economies make investments in capital, education, and technologies, thereby abstaining from consumption today, in order to increase consumption in the future. The DICE model extends this approach by including the "natural capital" of the climate system as an additional kind of capital stock. By devoting output to investments in natural capital through emissions reductions, reducing consumption today, economies prevent economically harmful climate change and thereby increase consumption possibilities in the future. In the model, different policies are evaluated on the basis of their contribution to the economic welfare (or, more precisely, consumption) of different generations.

The DICE model takes certain variables as given or assumed. These include, for each major region of the world, population, stocks of fossil fuels, and the pace of technological change. Most of the important variables are endogenous, or generated by the model. The endogenous variables include world output and capital stock, CO_2 emissions and concentrations, global temperature change, and climatic damages. Depending upon the policy investigated, the model also generates the policy response in terms of emissions reductions or carbon taxes (these are further discussed later). One of the shortcomings of the DICE model is that, as in most other integrated assessment models, technological change is exogenous rather than produced in response to changing market forces.

The DICE model is like an iceberg. The visible part contains a small number of mathematical equations that represent the laws of motion of output, emissions, climate change, and economic impacts. Yet beneath the surface, so to speak, these equations rest upon hundreds of studies of the individual components made by specialists in the natural and social sciences.

Good modeling practice in the area of climate change, as in any area, requires that the components of the model be accurate on the scale that is used. The DICE model contains a representation of each of the major components required for understanding climate change during the coming decades. Each of the components is a submodel that draws upon the research in that area. For example, the climate module uses the results of state-of-the-art climate models to project climate change as a function of GHG emissions. The impacts module draws upon the many studies of the impacts of climate change. The submodels used in the DICE model cannot produce the regional, industrial, and temporal details that are generated by the large specialized models. However, the small submodels have the advantage that, while striving to accurately represent the current state of knowledge, they can easily be modified. Most important, they are sufficiently concise that they can be incorporated into an integrated model that links all the major components.

For most of the submodels of the DICE model, such as those concerning climate or emissions, there are multiple approaches and sometimes heated controversies. In all cases, we have taken the scientific consensus for the appropriate models, parameters, or growth rates. In some cases, such as the long-run response of global mean temperature to a doubling of atmospheric CO_2, there is a long history of estimates and analyses of the uncertainties. In other areas, such as the impact of climate change on the economy, the central tendency and uncertainties are much less well understood, and we have less confidence in the assumptions. For example, the impacts of future climate change on low-probability but potentially catastrophic events, such as melting of the Greenland and Antarctic ice caps and a consequent rise in sea level of several meters, are imperfectly understood. The quantitative and policy implications of such uncertainties are addressed at the end of this summary.

The major advantage of using integrated assessment models like the DICE model is that questions about climate change can be answered in a consistent framework. The relationships that link economic growth, GHG emissions, the carbon cycle, the climate system, impacts and damages, and possible policies are exceedingly complex. It is extremely difficult to consider how changes in one part of the system will affect other parts of the system. For example, what will be the effect of higher economic growth on emissions and temperature trajectories? What will be the effect of higher fossil-fuel prices on climate change? How will the Kyoto Protocol or carbon taxes affect emissions, climate, and the economy? The purpose of integrated assessment models like the DICE model is not to provide definitive answers to these questions, for no definitive answers are possible, given the inherent uncertainties about many of the relationships. Rather, these models strive to make sure that the answers at least are internally consistent and at best provide a state-of-the-art description of the impacts of different forces and policies.

The Discount Rate

One economic concept that plays an important role in the analysis is the discount rate. In choosing among alternative trajectories for emissions reductions, we need to translate future costs into present values. We put present and future goods into a common currency by applying a discount rate on future goods. The discount rate is generally positive, but in situations of decline or depression it might be negative. Note also that the discount rate is calculated as a real discount rate on a bundle of goods and is net of inflation.

In general, we can think of the discount rate as the rate of return on capital investments. We can describe this concept by changing our one-commodity economy from corn to trees. Trees tomorrow (or, more generally, consumption tomorrow) have a different "price" than trees or consumption today because through production we can transform trees today into trees tomorrow. For example, if trees grow costlessly at a rate of 5 percent a year, then from a valuation point of view 105 trees a year from now is the economic equivalent of 100 trees today. That is, 100 trees today equal 105 trees tomorrow discounted by $1+.05$. Therefore, to compare different policies, we take the consumption flows for each policy and apply the appropriate discount rate. We then sum the discounted values for each period to get the total present value. Under the economic approach, if a stream of consumption has a higher present value under policy A than under policy B, then A is the preferred policy.

The choice of an appropriate discount rate is particularly important for climate-change policies because most of the impacts are far in the future. The approach in the DICE model is to use the estimated market return on capital as the discount rate. The estimated discount rate in the model averages 4 percent per year over the next century. This means that $1,000 worth of climate damages in a century is valued at $20 today. Although $20 may seem like a very small amount, it reflects the observation that capital is productive. Put differently, the discount rate is high to reflect the fact that investments in reducing future climate damages to corn and trees should compete with investments in better seeds, improved equipment, and other high-yield investments. With a higher discount rate, future damages look smaller, and we do less emissions reduction today; with a lower discount rate, future damages look larger, and we do more emissions reduction today. In thinking of long-run discounting, it is always useful to remember that the funds used to purchase Manhattan Island for $24 in 1626, when invested at a 4 percent real interest rate, would bring you the entire immense value of land in Manhattan today.

The Prices of Carbon Emissions and Carbon Taxes

Another key concept in the economics of climate change is the "carbon price," or, more precisely, the price that is attached to emissions of carbon dioxide. One version of a carbon price is the "social cost of carbon." This measures the cost of carbon emissions. More precisely, it is the present value of additional economic damages now and in the future caused by an additional ton of carbon emissions. We estimate that the social cost of carbon with no emissions limitations is today and in today's prices approximately $30 per ton of carbon for our standard set of assumptions. Therefore, in the automobile case discussed earlier, the total social cost or discounted damages from driving 10,000 miles would be $30, while the total social cost from the coal-generated electricity used by a typical U.S. household would be $90 per year. The annual social cost per capita of all CO_2 emissions for the United States would be about $150 per person (5 tons of carbon × $30 per ton). From an economic point of view, CO_2 emissions are an "externality," meaning that the driver or household is imposing these costs on the rest of the world today and in the future without paying the costs of these emissions.

In a situation where emissions are limited, it is useful to think of the market signal as a "carbon price." This represents the market price or penalty that would be paid by those who use the fossil fuels and thereby generate the CO_2 emissions. The carbon price might be imposed via a "carbon tax," which is like a gasoline tax or a cigarette tax except that it is levied on the carbon content of purchases. The units here are 2005 U.S. dollars per ton of carbon or CO_2. (Because of the different weights, to convert from dollars per ton of carbon to dollars per ton of CO_2 requires multiplying the dollars per ton of carbon by 3.67.) For example, if a country wished to impose a carbon tax of $30 per ton of carbon, this would involve a tax on gasoline of about 9 cents per gallon. Similarly, the tax on coal-generated electricity would be about 1 cent per kWh, or 10 percent of the current retail price. At current levels of carbon emissions in the United States, a tax of $30 per ton of carbon would generate $50 billion of revenue per year.

Another situation where a market price of carbon arises is in a "cap-and-trade" system. Cap-and-trade systems are the standard design for global-warming policies today, for example, under the Kyoto Protocol or under California's proposal for a state policy. Under this approach, total emissions are limited by governmental regulations (the cap), and emissions permits that sum to the total are allocated to firms and other entities or are auctioned. However, those who own the permits are allowed to sell them to others (the trade).

Trading emissions permits is one of the great innovations in environmental policy. The advantage of allowing trade is that some firms can reduce emissions more economically than others. If a firm has extremely high costs of reducing emissions, it is more efficient for that firm to purchase permits from firms whose emissions reductions can be made more inexpensively. This system has been widely used for environmental permits and is currently in use for CO_2 in the European Union (EU). As of the summer of 2007, permits in the EU were selling for about €20 per ton of CO_2, the equivalent of about $100 per ton of carbon.

Major Results

This book begins with an analysis of the likely future trajectory of the economy and the climate system if no significant emissions reductions are imposed, which we call the "baseline case." Our modeling projections indicate a rapid continued increase in CO_2 emissions from 7.4 billion tons of carbon per year in 2005 to 19 billion tons per year in 2100. The model's projected carbon emissions imply a rapid increase in atmospheric concentrations of CO_2 from 280 parts per million (ppm) in preindustrial times to 380 ppm in 2005 and to 685 ppm in 2100.

Measured mean global surface temperature in 2005 increased by 0.7°C relative to 1900 levels and is projected in the DICE model to increase by 3.1°C in 2100 relative to 1900. Although the longer-run future is subject to very great uncertainties, the DICE model's projected baseline increase in temperature for 2200 relative to 1900 is very large, 5.3°C. The climate changes associated with these temperature changes are estimated to increase damages by almost 3 percent of global output in 2100 and by close to 8 percent of global output in 2200.

This book analyzes a wide range of alternative policy responses to global warming. We start with an idealized policy that we label the "optimal" economic response. This is a policy in which all countries join to reduce GHG emissions in a fashion that is efficient across industries, countries, and time. The general principle behind the concept of the efficient policy is that the marginal costs of reducing CO_2 and other GHGs should be equalized in each sector and country; furthermore, in every year the marginal cost should be equal to the marginal benefit in lower future damages from climate change.

According to our estimates, efficient emissions reductions follow a "policy ramp" in which policies involve modest rates of emissions reductions in the near term, followed by sharp reductions in the medium and long terms. Our estimate of the optimal emissions-reduction rate for CO_2 relative to the baseline is 15 percent in the first policy period, increasing to 25 percent by 2050 and 45 percent by 2100. This path reduces CO_2 concentrations, and the increase in global mean temperature relative to 1900 is reduced to 2.6°C for 2100 and 3.4°C for 2200. (We pause to note that these calculations measure the emissions-reduction rates relative to the calculated baseline or no-controls emissions scenario. In most policy applications, the reductions are calculated relative to a historical baseline, such as, for the Kyoto Protocol, 1990 emissions levels. For example, when the German government proposed global emissions reductions of 50 percent by 2050 relative to 1990, this represented an 80 percent cut relative to the DICE model's calculated baseline because that baseline is projected to grow over the period from 1990 to 2050.)

The efficient climate-change policy would be relatively inexpensive and would have a substantial impact on long-run climate change. The net present-value global benefit of the optimal policy is $3 trillion relative to no controls. This total involves $2 trillion of abatement costs and $5 trillion of reduced climatic damages. Note that even after the optimal policy has been taken, there will still be substantial residual damages from climate change, which we estimate to be $17 trillion. More of the climate damages are not eliminated because the additional abatement would cost more than the additional reduction in damages.

An important result of the DICE model is to estimate the "optimal carbon price," or "optimal carbon tax." This is the price on carbon emissions that balances the incremental costs of reducing carbon emissions with the incremental benefits of reducing climate damages. We calculate that the economically optimal carbon price or carbon tax would be $27 per metric ton in 2005 in 2005 prices. (If prices are quoted in prices for carbon dioxide, which are smaller by a factor of 3.67, the optimal tax is $7.40 per ton of CO_2.)

We have examined several alternative approaches to global-warming policies. One important set of alternatives adds climatic constraints to the cost-benefit approach of the optimal policy. For example, these approaches might add a constraint that limits the atmospheric concentration of CO_2 to two times its preindustrial level. Alternatively, the constraint might limit the global temperature increase to 2.5°C. We found that for most of the climatic-limits cases, the net value of the policy is close to that of the optimal case. Moreover, the near-term carbon taxes that would apply to the climatic limits, except for the very stringent cases, are close to that of the economic optimum. For example, the 2005 carbon prices associated with CO_2 doubling and the 2.5°C increase are \$29 and \$31 per ton of carbon, respectively, compared with \$27 per ton for the pure optimum without climatic limits.

This book also shows that the trajectory of optimal carbon prices should rise sharply over the coming decades to reflect rising damages and the need for increasingly tight restraints. This is the policy ramp for carbon prices. The optimal price would rise steadily over time, at a rate between 2 and 3 percent per year in real terms, to reflect the rising damages from climate change. In the optimal trajectory, the carbon price would rise from \$27 per ton of carbon in the first period to \$90 per ton of carbon by 2050 and \$200 per ton of carbon in 2100.

The upper limit on the carbon price would be determined by the price at which all uses of fossil fuels can be economically replaced by other technologies. We designate this level as the cost of the backstop technology. We estimate that the upper limit will be around \$1,000 per ton of carbon over the next half century or so, but beyond that the projections for technological options are extremely difficult.

It should be emphasized that these prices are the best estimates, given current scientific and economic knowledge, and should be adjusted in accordance with new scientific information. Note as well that the price trajectory would involve a very substantial increase in the prices of fossil fuels over the longer run. For coal, a carbon tax of \$200 per ton would involve a coal-price increase of 200 to 400 percent depending upon the country, while for oil it would involve a price increase of about 30 percent relative to a price of \$60 per barrel. This sharp increase in the prices of fossil fuels is necessary to reduce their use and thereby reduce emissions. It also plays an important role in stimulating research, development, and investments in low-carbon or zero-carbon substitute energy sources.

The Importance of Efficient Policies

The results of this book emphatically point to the importance of designing cost-effective policies and avoiding inefficient policies. The term "cost-effective" denotes an approach that achieves a given objective at minimum cost. For example, it might be decided that a global temperature increase of 2.5°C is the maximum that can be safely allowed without setting in motion dangerous feedback effects. The economic approach is to find ways to achieve this objective with the lowest cost to the economy.

One important requirement—sometimes called "where-efficiency"—is that the marginal costs of emissions reductions be equalized across sectors and across countries. The only realistic way to achieve this is by imposing harmonized carbon prices that apply everywhere, with no exempted or favored sectors or excluded countries. One approach to price harmonization is universal carbon taxes. The second approach is a cap-and-trade system (or effectively linked multiple national cap-and-trade systems) in which all countries and sectors participate and all emissions are subject to trades.

A second requirement for efficiency is "when-efficiency," which requires that the timing of emissions reductions be efficiently designed. As described earlier, we estimate that the when-efficiency carbon price should rise between 2 and 3 percent per year in real terms. When-efficiency is much more difficult to estimate than where-efficiency because when-efficiency depends upon the discount rate and the dynamics of the carbon cycle and the climate system, as well as the economic damages from climate change.

All the policies that have been implemented to date fail the tests of where- and when-efficiency. The analyses in this book and several earlier studies indicate that the current Kyoto Protocol is seriously flawed in its environmental rationale, is inefficiently designed, and is likely to be ineffective. For example, in the current Kyoto Protocol, carbon prices are different across countries, ranging from relatively high in Europe to zero in the United States and developing countries. Moreover, within covered countries, some sectors are favored over others, and there is no mechanism to guarantee an efficient allocation over time. We estimate that the current Kyoto Protocol is extremely weak and inefficient without U.S. participation. It is only about 0.02 as effective as the optimal policy in reducing climatic damages and still incurs substantial abatement costs. Even if the United States were to join the current Kyoto Protocol, this approach would make only a small contribution to slowing global warming, and it would continue to be highly inefficient.

We have also analyzed several "ambitious" policies, such as the one proposed in 2007 by the German government, a proposal by Al Gore, and proposals generated using the objectives in the *Stern Review* (Stern 2007). For example, the 2007 Gore proposal for the United States was for a 90 percent reduction in CO_2 emissions below current levels by 2050, while the 2007 German proposal was to limit global CO_2 emissions in 2050 to 50 percent of 1990 levels. These proposals have the opposite problem to that of the current Kyoto Protocol. They are inefficient because they impose excessively large emissions reductions in the short run. According to the DICE model, they imply carbon taxes rising to around $300 per ton of carbon in the next two decades, and to the range of $600 to $800 per ton by midcentury. To return to our earlier examples, a $700 carbon tax would increase the price of coal-fired electricity in the United States by about 150 percent, and, at current levels of CO_2 emissions, it would impose a tax bill of $1,200 billion on the U.S. economy. From an economic point of view, such a high carbon tax would prove much more expensive than necessary to achieve a given climate objective.

Our modeling results point to the importance of near-universal participation in programs to reduce greenhouse gases. Because of the structure of the costs of abatement, with marginal costs being very low for the initial reductions but rising sharply for higher reductions, there are substantial excess costs if the preponderance of sectors and countries are not fully included. We preliminarily estimate that a participation rate of 50 percent, as compared with 100 percent, will impose an abatement-cost penalty of 250 percent. Even with the participation of the top 15 countries and regions, consisting of three-quarters of world emissions, we estimate that the cost penalty is about 70 percent.

We have determined that a low-cost and environmentally benign substitute for fossil fuels would be highly beneficial. In other words, a low-cost backstop technology would have substantial economic benefits. We estimate that such a low-cost zero-carbon technology would have a net value of around $17 trillion in present value because it would allow the globe to avoid most of the damages from climate change. No such technology presently exists, and we can only speculate on it. It might be low-cost solar power, geothermal energy, some nonintrusive climatic engineering, or genetically engineered carbon-eating trees. Although none of these options is currently feasible, the net benefits of zero-carbon substitutes are so high as to warrant very intensive research.

The Necessity of Raising Carbon Prices

Economics contains one fundamental inconvenient truth about climate-change policy: For any policy to be effective in slowing global warming, it must raise the market price of carbon, which will raise the prices of fossil fuels and the products of fossil fuels. Prices can be raised by limiting the number of carbon-emissions permits that are available (cap-and-trade) or by levying a tax (or some euphemism such as a "climate damage charge") on carbon emissions. Economics teaches us that it is unrealistic to hope that major reductions in emissions can be achieved by hope, trust, responsible citizenship, environmental ethics, or guilt alone. The only way to have major and durable effects on such a large sector for millions of firms and billions of people and trillions of dollars of expenditure is to raise the price of carbon emissions.

Raising the price of carbon will achieve four goals. First, it will provide signals to consumers about what goods and services are high-carbon ones and should therefore be used more sparingly. Second, it will provide signals to producers about which inputs use more carbon (such as coal and oil) and which use less or none (such as natural gas or nuclear power), thereby inducing firms to substitute low-carbon inputs. Third, it will give market incentives for inventors and innovators to develop and introduce low-carbon products and processes that can replace the current generation of technologies.

Fourth, and most important, a high carbon price will economize on the information that is required to do all three of these tasks. Through the market mechanism, a high carbon price will raise the price of products according to their carbon content. Ethical consumers today, hoping to minimize their "carbon footprint," have little chance of making an accurate calculation of the relative carbon use in, say, driving 250 miles as compared with flying 250 miles. A harmonized carbon tax would raise the price of a good proportionately to exactly the amount of CO_2 that is emitted in all the stages of production that are involved in producing that good. If 0.01 of a ton of carbon emissions results from the wheat growing and the milling and the trucking and the baking of a loaf of bread, then a tax of $30 per ton carbon will raise the price of bread by $0.30. The "carbon footprint" is automatically calculated by the price system. Consumers would still not know how much of the price is due to carbon emissions, but they could make their decisions confident that they are paying for the social cost of their carbon footprint.

Because of the political unpopularity of taxes, it is tempting to use subsidies for "clean" or "green" technologies as a substitute for raising the price of carbon emissions. This is an economic and environmental snare to be avoided. The fundamental problem is that there are too many clean activities to subsidize. Virtually everything from market bicycles to nonmarket walking has a low carbon intensity relative to driving. There are simply insufficient resources to subsidize all activities that are low emitters. Even if the resources were available, the calculation of an appropriate subsidy for a particular activity would be a horrendously complicated task. An additional problem is that the existence of subsidies encourages a pell-mell race for benefits—an environmental form of rent-seeking activity. Ethanol subsidies in the United States, which are rapidly turning into an economic nightmare by diverting precious agricultural resources to the inefficient production of energy, are a case study in the folly of subsidies. To some extent, subsidies are simply the attempt of those who have the responsibility to clean up their activities by reducing emissions to place the fiscal burden elsewhere. Finally, subsidies have the public-finance problem of requiring revenues, which would involve raising the inefficiency of the tax system.

There are exceptions to the general rule to avoid subsidies in combating global warming. It is economically appropriate to subsidize activities such as invention, innovation, and education—which are public goods rather than public bads—through government funding or tax credits. For example, the tax credit on research and development and government funding of basic research in energy science are appropriate uses of the subsidy approach. But these are the economic opposites of harmful activities such as the burning of fossil fuels.

Whether someone is serious about tackling the global-warming problem can be readily gauged by listening to what he or she says about the carbon price. Suppose you hear a public figure who speaks eloquently of the perils of global warming and proposes that the nation should move urgently to slow climate change. Suppose that person proposes regulating the fuel efficiency of cars, or requiring high-efficiency lightbulbs, or subsidizing ethanol, or providing research support for solar power—but nowhere does the proposal raise the price of carbon. You should conclude that the proposal is not really serious and does not recognize the central economic message about how to slow climate change. To a first approximation, raising the price of carbon is a necessary and sufficient step for tackling global warming. The rest is at best rhetoric and may actually be harmful in inducing economic inefficiencies.

The Advantage of Carbon Taxes and Price-Type Approaches

If an effective climate-change policy requires raising the market price of carbon emissions, then there are two alternative approaches for doing so. The first is a price-type approach such as carbon taxes, and the second is a quantity-type approach such as the cap-and-trade systems that are envisioned in the Kyoto Protocol and most other policy proposals.

It is worth pausing here to describe an international system for the price-type alternative. One approach is called "harmonized carbon taxes." Under this approach, all countries would agree to penalize carbon emissions in all sectors at an internationally harmonized carbon price or carbon tax. The carbon price might be determined by estimates of the price necessary to limit GHG concentrations or temperature changes below some level thought to trigger "dangerous interferences" with the climatic system (this is the term used in the United Nations Framework Convention on Climate Change as a goal of international climate policy). Alternatively, it might be the price that would induce the estimated "optimal" level of control. The results of this book suggest, as stated earlier, a tax of around $27 per ton of carbon at present, rising at between 2 and 3 percent per year in real terms. Because carbon prices would be equalized across countries and sectors, this approach would satisfy where-efficiency. If the carbon-tax trajectory grows at the appropriate rate, it will also satisfy the rules for when-efficiency.

We have examined the relative advantages of the two regimes and conclude that price-type approaches have many advantages. One advantage of carbon taxes is that they can more easily and flexibly integrate the economic costs and benefits of emissions reductions. The quantity-type approach in the Kyoto Protocol has no discernible connection with ultimate environmental or economic goals, although some recent revisions, such as the 2007 German proposal, are linked to global temperature objectives. The advantage of a price-type approach is emphatically reinforced by the large uncertainties and evolving scientific knowledge in this area. Emissions taxes are more efficient in the face of massive uncertainties because of the relative linearity of the benefits compared with the costs. Quantitative limits will produce high volatility in the market price of carbon under an emissions-targeting approach, as has already been seen in the EU's cap-and-trade system for CO_2.

In addition, a tax approach allows the public to get the revenues from restrictions more easily than allocational quantitative approaches, and it may therefore be seen as fairer and can minimize the distortions caused by the tax system. Because taxes raise revenues (whereas allocations give the revenues to the recipient), the public revenues can be used to soften the economic impacts on lower-income households, to fund necessary research on low-carbon energy, and to help poor countries move away from high-carbon fuels. The tax approach also provides less opportunity for corruption and financial finagling than quantitative limits because a price-type approach creates no artificial scarcities to encourage rent-seeking behavior.

It should be noted that many recent successors to the Kyoto Protocol that are being discussed propose auctioning some or all of the emissions permits. This is an important innovation, for auctions raise revenues and therefore can have the advantageous effect on tax efficiency of a carbon tax. Moreover, there is a temptation in tax systems to grant exemptions, thereby reducing their environmental integrity and cost-effectiveness, and quantitative systems have often been more successful in being comprehensive within a country. The major point to emphasize here is that whichever approach is taken—quantitative or tax-based—the public should capture the revenues through taxes or auctions, and there should be an absolute minimum of exemptions.

Carbon taxes have the apparent disadvantage that they do not steer the world economy toward a particular climatic target, such as either a CO_2 concentration or a global temperature limit. People might worry that we need quantitative emissions limits to ensure that the globe remains on the safe side of "dangerous interferences" with the climate system. However, this advantage of quantitative limits is probably illusory. We do not currently know what emissions levels would actually lead to dangerous interferences, or even if there are dangerous interferences. We might make a huge mistake—either on the high or the low side—and impose much too rigid and expensive, or much too lax, quantitative limits. In other words, whatever initial target we set is likely to prove incorrect for either taxes or quantities. The major question is whether it would prove easier to make periodic large adjustments to incorrectly set harmonized carbon taxes or to incorrectly set negotiated emissions limits.

We conclude that more emphasis should be placed on including price-type features in climate-change policy rather than relying solely on quantity-type approaches such as cap-and-trade schemes. A middle ground between the two is a hybrid, called the "cap-and-tax" system, in which quantitative limits are buttressed by a carbon tax along with a safety valve that prevents excessively high carbon prices. An example of a hybrid plan would be a cap-and-trade system with an initial carbon tax of $30 per ton along with a provision for firms to purchase additional permits at a penalty price of $45 per ton of carbon. This hybrid plan would combine some of the advantages of both price and quantity approaches.

Tax Bads Rather than Goods

Taxes are almost a four-letter word in the American political lexicon. But the discussion of taxes sometimes makes a fundamental mistake in failing to distinguish between different kinds of taxes. Some people have objected to carbon taxes because, they argue, taxes lead to economic inefficiencies. While this analysis is generally correct for taxes on "goods" like consumption, labor, and savings, it is incorrect for taxes on "bads" like CO_2 emissions.

Taxes on labor distort people's decisions about how much to work and when to retire, and these distortions can be costly to the economy. Taxes on bads like CO_2 are precisely the opposite; they serve to remove implicit subsidies on harmful or wasteful activities. Allowing people to emit CO_2 into the atmosphere for free is similar to allowing people to smoke in a crowded room or dump trash in a national park. Carbon taxes therefore enhance efficiency because they correct market distortions that arise when people do not take into account the external effects of their energy consumption. If the economy could replace inefficient taxes on goods like food and leisure with efficient taxes on bads like carbon emissions, there would be significant improvements in economic efficiency.

Two Cautionary Notes

We close with two cautionary notes. First, it is important to recognize that this book represents only one perspective on how to approach climate change. It is a limited perspective because it uses economics to examine alternative approaches, and it is further narrowed because it represents the viewpoint of one person with all the blinders, cognitive constraints, and biases involved in individual research. There are many other perspectives through which to analyze approaches for slowing global warming. These perspectives differ in normative assumptions, estimated behavioral structures, scientific data and modeling, levels of aggregation, treatment of uncertainty, and disciplinary background. No sensible policymaker would base the globe's future on a single model, a single set of computer runs, a single viewpoint, or a single national, ethical, or disciplinary perspective. Sensible decision making requires a robust set of alternative scenarios and sensitivity analyses. But this is the role of committees and panels, not of individual scholars.

A second reservation concerns the profound uncertainties that are involved at every stage of modeling global warming. We are uncertain about the growth of output over the next century and beyond, about what energy systems will be developed in the decades ahead, about the pace of technological change in substitutes for carbon fuels or in carbon-removal technologies, about the climatic reaction to rising concentrations of GHGs, and perhaps most of all about the economic and ecological responses to a changing climate.

This book takes the standard economic approach to uncertainty known as the expected utility model, which relies on an assessment with subjective or judgmental probabilities. This approach uses the best available information on the level and uncertainties for the major variables to determine how the presence of uncertainty might change our policies relative to a best-guess policy. (The "best guess" is shorthand for basing our model on the mean or expected values of the parameters of the model.) This approach assumes that there are no genuinely catastrophic outcomes that would wipe out the human species or destroy the fabric of human civilizations. Estimating the likelihood of, and dealing with, potentially catastrophic outcomes is one of the continuing important subjects of research for the natural and social sciences.

Based on the expected utility model, one finding of the uncertainty analysis in this book is that the best-guess policy is a good approximation to the expected-value policy. There appears to be no empirical ground for paying a major risk premium for future uncertainties beyond what would be justified by the averages (subject to the caveats about catastrophic outcomes in the preceding paragraph).

At the same time, we must emphasize that, based on our formal analysis of uncertainty, we have relatively little confidence in our projections beyond 2050. For example, in our uncertainty analysis, we project the "two-sigma" error bands for several variables on the basis of scientific and economic uncertainties about the various parameters and systems (the two-sigma error band is the range within which we believe the true figure lies with 68 percent confidence). Our estimate is that the two-sigma band for global mean temperature increase by 2100 is 1.9°C to 4.1°C. A similar calculation for the current social cost of carbon in the baseline projection lies between $10 and $41 per ton of carbon. These pervasive uncertainties are one of the most difficult features of dealing with climate change.

The final message of this book is a simple one: Global warming is a serious problem that will not solve itself. Countries should take cooperative steps to slow global warming. There is no case for delay. The most fruitful and effective approach is for countries to put a harmonized price—perhaps a steep price—on greenhouse-gas emissions, primarily those of carbon dioxide resulting from the combustion of fossil fuels. Although other measures might usefully buttress this policy, placing a near-universal and harmonized price or tax on carbon is a necessary and perhaps even a sufficient condition for reducing the future threat of global warming.

II
Background and Description of the DICE Model

General Background on Global Warming

Before getting into modeling details, it will be useful to sketch the scientific basis for concerns about global warming, as reviewed by the IPCC's *Climate Change 2007: The Physical Science Basis* (IPCC 2007b). As a result of the buildup of atmospheric greenhouse gases (GHGs), it is expected that significant climate changes will occur in the coming decades and beyond. The major industrial GHGs are carbon dioxide (CO_2), methane, ozone, nitrous oxides, and chlorofluorocarbons (CFCs).

The most important GHG is CO_2, whose emissions have risen rapidly in recent decades. The atmospheric concentration of carbon dioxide of 380 parts per million (ppm) in 2005 far exceeds the range over the past 650,000 years (estimated to be between 180 and 300 ppm). Current calculations from climate models are that doubling the amount of CO_2 or the equivalent in the atmosphere compared with preindustrial levels will in equilibrium lead to an increase in the global surface temperature of 2 to 4.5°C, with a best estimate of about 3°C. The suite of models and emissions scenarios used by the IPCC produces a range of temperature change over the twenty-first century of between 1.8 and 4.0°C. Other projected effects are increases in precipitation and evaporation, an increase in extreme events such as hurricanes, and a rise in sea levels of 0.2 to 0.6 meters during this century. Some models also predict regional shifts, such as hotter and drier climates in midcontinental regions, such as the U.S. Midwest. Climate monitoring indicates that actual global warming is occurring in line with scientific predictions.[1]

Although scientists have been analyzing global warming for more than half a century, nations took the first formal steps to slow global warming about 15 years ago under the United Nations Framework Convention on Climate Change. The first binding international agreement on climate change, the Kyoto Protocol, came into effect in 2005, and the first period for emissions reductions, 2008–2012, is at hand. The framework for implementing the Protocol is most solidly institutionalized in the European Union's Emissions Trading Scheme (EU ETS; European Commission 2006), which covers almost half of Europe's CO_2 emissions.[2]

Notwithstanding its successful implementation, the Kyoto Protocol is widely seen as a troubled institution. Early problems appeared with the failure to include the major developing countries, the lack of an agreed-upon mechanism to include new countries, and an agreement that is limited to a single period. The major blow came when the United States withdrew from the treaty in 2001. Whereas 66 percent of 1990 world emissions were included in the original Protocol, that number declined to 32 percent in 2002 with the withdrawal of the United States and strong economic growth in excluded countries, largely the developing nations of the world. Strict enforcement of the Kyoto Protocol is likely to be observed primarily in those countries and industries covered by the EU ETS, and their emissions today account for only about 8 percent of the global total. If the current Protocol is extended at current emissions levels, models indicate that it will have little impact on global climate change.[3]

Nations are now beginning to consider the structure of climate-change policies for the period after 2008–2012. Some countries, states, cities, companies, and even universities are adopting their own climate-change policies. Most global-warming policies adopted by U.S. states or considered by the U.S. federal government contain some mixture of emissions limits and technology standards. Is the Kyoto Protocol a viable long-term approach to this long-term problem? Are there alternatives that might reduce global warming more efficiently? What are the costs and benefits of alternative approaches? I consider these questions in this book.

Economic Sectors in the DICE-2007 Model

We next turn to a verbal description of the DICE-2007 model, after which we provide the detailed equations.[4] The DICE model views the economics of climate change from the perspective of neoclassical economic growth theory. In this approach, economies make investments in capital, education, and technologies, thereby abstaining from consumption today, in order to increase consumption in the future. The DICE model extends this approach by including the "natural capital" of the climate system as an additional kind of capital stock. In other words, we can view concentrations of GHGs as negative natural capital, and emissions reductions as investments that raise the quantity of natural capital. By devoting output to emissions reductions, economies reduce consumption today but prevent economically harmful climate change and thereby increase consumption possibilities in the future.

The DICE model is a global model that aggregates different countries into a single level of output, capital stock, technology, and emissions. The estimates for the global aggregates are built up from data that include all major countries, and the specification allows for differentiated responses and technological growth. A parallel research effort, jointly with Zili Yang, is devoted to a multiregion version of the DICE model. That effort is called the RICE model (for Regional Integrated model of Climate and the Economy). The advantage of the DICE model is that the basic trends and trade-offs can be captured reasonably accurately, and the underlying model is much more transparent and easily modified by researchers.

In the DICE model, the world is assumed to have a well-defined set of preferences, represented by a "social welfare function," which ranks different paths of consumption. The social welfare function is increasing in the per capita consumption of each generation, with diminishing marginal utility of consumption. The importance of a generation's per capita consumption depends on the size of the population. The relative importance of different generations is affected by two central normative parameters: the pure rate of time preference and the elasticity of the marginal utility of consumption (the "consumption elasticity" for short). These two parameters interact to determine the discount rate on goods, which is critical for intertemporal economic choices. In the modeling, we set the parameters to be consistent with observed economic outcomes as reflected by interest rates and rates of return on capital.

The consumption path is constrained by both economic and geophysical relationships. The economy has two major decision variables in the model: the overall savings rate for physical capital and the emissions-control rate for greenhouse gases.

We begin with the standard neoclassical decisions about capital accumulation and then consider the geophysical constraints. There is a single commodity, which can be used for either consumption or investment. Consumption should be viewed broadly to include not only food and shelter but also nonmarket environmental amenities and services. Each region is endowed with initial stocks of capital and labor and an initial and region-specific level of technology. Population growth and technological change are region-specific and exogenous, while capital accumulation is determined by optimizing the flow of consumption over time. Regional outputs and capital stocks are aggregated using purchasing-power-parity (PPP) exchange rates.

Output is produced by a Cobb-Douglas production function in capital, labor, and energy. Energy takes the form of either carbon-based fuels (such as coal) or non-carbon-based technologies (such as solar or geothermal energy or nuclear power). Technological change takes two forms: economy-wide technological change and carbon-saving technological change. Carbon-saving technological change is modeled as reducing the ratio of CO_2 emissions to output. Both forms of technological change are exogenous in the current version of the DICE model. This is a serious limitation, particularly for carbon-saving technological change, because changing carbon prices are likely to induce research and development on new energy technologies. However, robust modeling of induced technological change has proven extremely difficult, and to date no reliable modeling specification for a DICE-type model has been developed.

Carbon fuels are limited in supply. Substitution of non-carbon fuels for carbon fuels takes place over time as carbon-based fuels become more expensive, either because of resource exhaustion or because policies are taken to limit carbon emissions. One of the new features of this round of the DICE model is an explicit inclusion of a backstop technology for noncarbon energy. This technology allows for the complete replacement of all carbon fuels at a price that is relatively high but declines over time.

Geophysical Sectors

The major differentiating feature of the DICE model is the inclusion of several geophysical relationships that link the economy with the different factors affecting climate change. These relationships include the carbon cycle, a radiative-forcing equation, climate-change equations, and a climate-damage relationship.

In the DICE-2007 model, the only GHG that is subject to controls is industrial CO_2. This reflects the view that CO_2 is the major contributor to global warming and that other GHGs are likely to be controlled in different ways (chlorofluorocarbons are a useful example). Other GHGs are included as exogenous trends in radiative forcing; these include primarily CO_2 emissions from land-use changes, other well-mixed GHGs, and aerosols.

CO_2 emissions are projected as a function of total output, a time-varying emissions-output ratio, and an emissions-control rate. The emissions-output ratio is estimated for individual regions and is then aggregated to the global ratio. The emissions-control rate is determined by the climate-change policy under examination. The cost of emissions reductions is parameterized by a log-linear function that is calibrated to recent studies of the cost of emissions reductions.

The carbon cycle is based upon a three-reservoir model calibrated to existing carbon-cycle models and historical data. We assume that there are three reservoirs for carbon: the atmosphere, a quickly mixing reservoir in the upper oceans and the biosphere, and the deep oceans. Carbon flows in both directions between adjacent reservoirs. The mixing between the deep oceans and other reservoirs is extremely slow.

The climate equations are a simplified representation that includes an equation for radiative forcing and two equations for the climate system. The radiative-forcing equation calculates the impact of the accumulation of GHGs on the radiation balance of the globe. The climate equations calculate the mean surface temperature of the globe and the average temperature of the deep oceans for each time-step. These equations draw upon and are calibrated to large-scale general circulation models of the atmosphere and ocean systems. The structure of these equations is largely unchanged from earlier DICE models, although the parameters have been updated and the timing has been refined.

The final issue involves the economic impact of climate change, which is thorniest issue in climate-change economics. Estimates of economic impacts are indispensable for making sensible decisions about the appropriate balance between costly emissions reductions and climate damages. However, providing reliable estimates of the damages from climate change over the long run has proven extremely difficult. This book relies on estimates from earlier syntheses of the damages, with updates in light of more recent information. The basic assumption is that the damages from gradual and small climate changes are modest, but the damages rise nonlinearly with the extent of climate change. These estimates also assume that the damages are likely to be relatively larger for poor, small, and tropical countries than for rich, large, and midlatitude countries.

III

Derivation of the Equations of the DICE-2007 Model

This chapter presents the mathematical structure of the DICE-2007 model. We begin with the objective function, next present the economic relationships, and end with the geophysical equations. The major changes since the last generation of RICE-DICE models are described in the last part of the chapter. The equations of the DICE-2007 model are listed in the Appendix. We will refer to the Appendix equations as we proceed with this discussion.

Before beginning this technical description, we should note that our research was undertaken primarily on the basis of the Third Assessment Reports of the IPCC but before the landmark Fourth Assessment Reports of the IPCC were published. Some of the modeling was informed by the "Summary for Policymakers" (IPCC 2007a), and the full report on science (IPCC 2007b) was reviewed before the final draft was prepared. As of the final draft, the full reports on impacts and mitigation were not available.

Objective Function

The DICE model assumes that economic and climate policies should be designed to optimize the flow of consumption over time. Consumption should be interpreted as "generalized consumption," which includes not only traditional market goods and services like food and shelter but also nonmarket items such as leisure, health status, and environmental services.

The mathematical representation of this assumption is that policies are chosen to maximize a social welfare function that is the discounted sum of the population-weighted utility of per capita consumption. Equation (A.1) is the mathematical statement of the objective function. This representation is a standard one in modern theories of optimal economic growth.

A number of further assumptions underlie this choice of an objective function. First, it involves a specific representation of the value or "utility" of consumption. Equation (A.3) shows that the utility in each period is an isoelastic function of per capita consumption. This form assumes a constant elasticity of the marginal utility of consumption, α. We calibrate α in conjunction with the pure rate of time preference, as discussed later. Second, this specification assumes that the value of consumption in a period is proportional to the population. Third, this approach applies a discount on the economic well-being of future generations, as is defined in equation (A.2). In this specification, we designate the pure rate of social time preference, ρ, as the discount rate that provides the welfare weights of the utilities of different generations. This specification is different from that in earlier DICE-RICE models, as is explained in the next section.

We should add a note about interpretation of the equilibrium in the DICE model. We have specified the baseline or no-controls case so that, from a conceptual point of view, it represents the outcome of market and policy factors as they currently exist. In other words, the baseline model is an attempt to project from a positive perspective the levels and growth of major economic and environmental variables as they would occur with no climate-change policies. Putting this in technical language, the prices and incomes in the baseline run should be interpreted as "Negishi prices and incomes," which means that they are prices and incomes that are consistent with the competitive-market equilibrium. The analysis does not make any case for the social desirability of the distribution of incomes over space or time of existing conditions, any more than a marine biologist makes a moral judgment on the equity of the eating habits of marine organisms.

The calculations of the potential improvements in world welfare from efficient climate-change policies examine potential improvements within the context of the existing distribution of income and investments across space and time. There may be other improvements—in environmental policies, in military policies, in tax or transfer programs, or in international aid programs—that would improve the human condition, perhaps even more than the policies we consider. To make improvements in the area studied here does not deny injustice, inequality, or folly in other areas or the scope for other policies. But we must limit the scope of this book to what is already a sufficiently complex area.

Economic Variables

The next set of equations determines the evolution of world output over time. Population and the labor force are exogenous. These are simplified to logistic-type equations in which the growth of population in the first decade is given and the growth rate declines so that total population approaches a limit of 8.5 billion. This is slightly below the middle estimate of the United Nations' long-term projection, but it is calibrated to match the recent stochastic International Institute of Applied Systems Analysis (IIASA) projections.[1]

Production is represented by a modification of a standard neoclassical production function. The underlying population and output estimates are aggregated from a 12-region model. Outputs are measured in purchasing-power-parity (PPP) exchange rates using International Monetary Fund (IMF) estimates.[2] Total output for each region is projected using a partial convergence model, and the outputs are then aggregated to the world total. The regional and global production functions are assumed to be constant-returns-to-scale Cobb-Douglas production functions in capital, labor, and Hicks-neutral technological change. The global aggregate is shown in equation (A.4) as follows:

$$(A.4) \quad Q(t) = \Omega(t)[1 - \Lambda(t)]A(t)K(t)^{\gamma}L(t)^{1-\gamma}$$

The additional variables in the production function are $\Omega(t)$ and $\Lambda(t)$, which represent climate damages and abatement costs, shown in equations (A.5) and (A.6). The damage function assumes that damages are proportional to world output and are polynomial functions of global mean temperature change. The aggregate damage curve is built up from estimates of the damages of the 12 regions, including assumed sectoral change and underlying income elasticities of different outputs. It includes estimated damages to major sectors such as agriculture, the cost of sea-level rise, adverse impacts on health, and nonmarket damages, as well as estimates of the potential costs of catastrophic damages.[3] It is clear that this equation is extremely conjectural, given the thin base of empirical studies on which it rests.

The abatement-cost equation is a reduced-form-type model in which the costs of emissions reductions are a function of the emissions-reduction rate, $\mu(t)$. The abatement-cost function assumes that abatement costs are proportional to global output and to a polynomial function of the reduction rate. The cost function is estimated to be highly convex, indicating that the marginal cost of reductions rises from zero more than linearly with the reductions rate.

A new feature of the DICE-2007 model is that it explicitly includes a backstop technology, which is a technology that can replace all fossil fuels. The backstop technology could be one that removes carbon from the atmosphere or an all-purpose environmentally benign zero-carbon energy technology. It might be solar power, or nuclear-based hydrogen, or some as-yet-undiscovered source. The backstop price is assumed to be initially high and to decline over time with carbon-saving technological change. The backstop technology is introduced into the model by setting the time path of the parameters in the abatement-cost equation (A.6) so that the marginal cost of abatement at a control rate of 100 percent is equal to the backstop price for each year.[4]

The next three equations, (A.7) through (A.9), are standard accounting equations that include the definition of consumption, per capita consumption, and the capital balance equation. The final two equations in the economic block are the emissions equation and the resource constraint on carbon fuels. Uncontrolled industrial CO_2 emissions in equation (A.10) are given by a level of carbon intensity, $\sigma(t)$, times world output. Actual emissions are then reduced by the emissions-reduction rate, $\mu(t)$, described earlier. The carbon intensity is taken to be exogenous and is built up from emissions estimates of the 12 regions, whereas the emissions-reduction rate is the control variable in the different experiments. Equation (A.11) is a limitation on total resources of carbon fuels. The DICE model assumes that incremental extraction costs are zero and that carbon fuels are optimally allocated over time by the market, producing the optimal Hotelling rents.

Geophysical Equations

The next equations (A.12 to A.18) link economic activity and greenhouse-gas emissions to the carbon cycle, radiative forcings, and climate change. These relationships have proved a major challenge because of the need to simplify what are inherently complex dynamics into a small number of equations that can be used in an integrated economic-geophysical model. As with the economics, the modeling philosophy for the geophysical relationships has been to use parsimonious specifications so that the theoretical model is transparent and the optimization model is empirically and computationally tractable.

Equation (A.12) provides the relationship between economic activity and greenhouse-gas emissions. In the DICE-2007 model, only industrial CO_2 emissions are endogenous. The other GHGs (including CO_2 arising from land-use changes) are exogenous and are projected on the basis of studies by other modeling groups.

The carbon cycle is represented by a three-reservoir model calibrated to existing carbon-cycle models, similar to the treatment in DICE/RICE-1999. There are three reservoirs for carbon: the atmosphere, a quickly mixing reservoir in the upper oceans and the biosphere, and the deep oceans. The deep oceans provide a finite, albeit vast, sink for carbon in the long run. Each of the three reservoirs is assumed to be well mixed in the short run, while the mixing between the upper reservoirs and the deep oceans is assumed to be extremely slow. Equations (A.13) through (A.15) are the equations of the carbon cycle. These equations have been modified since the last round to remove a problem with the lag structure. We have calibrated the parameters to match the carbon cycle in the Model for the Assessment of Greenhouse Gas Induced Climate Change (MAGICC).[5]

The next step concerns the relationship between the accumulation of GHGs and climate change. These equations use the same specifications as the original DICE/RICE models. Climate modelers have developed a wide variety of approaches for estimating the impact of rising GHGs on climatic variables. On the whole, existing research models are much too complex to be included in economic models, particularly ones that are used for optimization. Instead, we employ a small structural model that captures the basic relationship between GHG concentrations, radiative forcing, and the dynamics of climate change.

Accumulations of GHGs lead to warming at the earth's surface through increases in radiative forcing. The relationship between GHG accumulations and increased radiative forcing is derived from empirical measurements and climate models, as shown in equation (A.16). The major part of warming is due to CO_2, while the balance is exogenous forcing from other long-lived greenhouse gases, aerosols, ozone, and other factors. The DICE model treats other greenhouse gases and forcing components as exogenous because these are relatively small and their control is either exogenous (as in the case of CFCs) or poorly understood (as with cloud albedo effects). We have slightly adjusted the forcing parameter for CO_2 from earlier DICE models, but this has little effect on the results.

The next set of relationships is the climate model. The specification in equations (A.17) and (A.18) is similar to the original DICE/RICE models. Higher radiative forcing warms the atmospheric layer, which then warms the upper ocean and gradually the deep ocean. The lags in the system are primarily caused by the diffusive inertia of the different layers. We have changed the timing slightly to improve the match of the impulse-response function with climate models. Additionally, we have adjusted the climate sensitivity to the center of the IPCC range of 3°C for an equilibrium CO_2 doubling. The timing is calibrated to match model experiments for the IPCC Third and Fourth Assessment Reports. In addition, the parameters are calibrated so that the forcing leads to the same temperature trajectory over the twenty-first century as do the MAGICC model simulations.[6] The DICE-model climate module tends to overpredict the historical temperature change, given estimates of emissions and forcing, but matches the projections from the IPCC scenarios, particularly the high-emissions scenarios such as A1F1, as well as the MAGICC simulations.

Computational Considerations

The computations for the DICE-2007 model use the CONOPT solver in the GAMS modeling system.[7] This is based on the generalized reduced gradient (GRG) algorithm. The basic approach is to embed a linear programming algorithm inside an algorithm that linearizes the nonlinear equations. Although this algorithm does not guarantee that the solution is the global optimum, our experience over the years has not suggested any solutions other than those found by the algorithm. The model used here involves 1,263 equations and 1,381 variables. The runs take approximately 30 seconds using a 3.0 GHz Intel processor. It should be noted that the DICE problem is conceptually a mathematical optimization problem rather than the standard recursive time-stepped problem often used in the natural sciences; optimization requires special tools and takes much longer than recursive calculation of a similarly sized problem.

Revisions since DICE-1999

The DICE-2007 model is the fifth generation of the aggregated global dynamic model. For those who are familiar with earlier versions, particularly Nordhaus 1994 and Nordhaus and Boyer 2000, this section describes the major revisions.[8]

DATA INPUTS

All the economic and geophysical data have been updated, and the new first period is centered on 2005. The first period for the last full revision of the model (in Nordhaus and Boyer 2000) was centered on 1995. Economic data for the current revision use IMF estimates for major economic aggregates with preliminary data from 2005. Energy data are from the World Bank and U.S. Energy Information Agency (EIA). Carbon dioxide emissions are from the EIA and the Carbon Dioxide Information Analysis Center. Geophysical data are from multiple sources, including primarily the Goddard Institute for Space Studies and the Hadley Centre. The revision incorporates some results from the IPCC Fourth Assessment Report, as well as more comprehensive revisions from the IPCC

Third Assessment Report. Data on CO_2 emissions generally go through 2004, with some preliminary data for 2005 and 2006. Prices have been updated to 2005 U.S. dollars. The conceptual basis for outputs has been changed from market exchange rates to purchasing-power-parity (PPP) exchange rates.[9]

REGIONAL AGGREGATION ALONG WITH ECONOMIC AND EMISSIONS PROJECTIONS

The economic, emissions, and impact estimates are based on 12 regions and are then aggregated to the global total using PPP exchange rates. The 12 regions are the United States, the European Union, other high-income countries, Russia, Eastern Europe and the non-Russian former Soviet Union, Japan, China, India, the Middle East, sub-Saharan Africa, Latin America, and other Asia. Estimates for each region are built up from data on the 71 largest countries. These countries represent 97 percent of emissions, 94 percent of world output, and 86 percent of population. For each region, we project population, output, carbon intensity, and baseline CO_2 emissions by decade. We then aggregate to the global total for each year. Figure 3-1 shows the historical emissions-output ratios for five important regions and the global total, displaying a steady decarbonization after 1960. However, the most recent trend is for a stable global CO_2-GDP ratio, due in part to the rise in CO_2 emissions from China.

Figure 3-2 shows the emissions projections for the baseline run of the DICE-2007 model along with those from several "SRES scenarios" developed in the *Special Report on Emissions Scenarios* for the IPCC (IPCC 2000). The DICE-model projections are developed completely independently using different

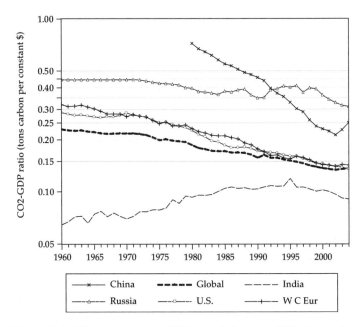

Figure 3-1. Historical ratios of CO_2 emissions to GDP for major regions and globe, 1960–2004. Trends in the ratio of CO_2 emissions to GDP for five major regions and the global total. We call the decline in this rate "decarbonization." Most major economies have had significant decarbonization since 1960. The rates of decarbonization have slowed or reversed in the last few years and appear to have reversed for China. With the changing composition of output by region, the world CO_2-GDP ratio has remained stable since 2000. Note that "W C Eur" is Western and central Europe and includes several formerly centrally planned countries with high CO_2-GDP ratios.

methods and more recent data (the SRES scenarios used in the latest IPCC projections were developed approximately a decade ago). The DICE emissions projection is toward the low end of the SRES range until the middle of the twenty-first century and then rises relative to some of the lower SRES scenarios.

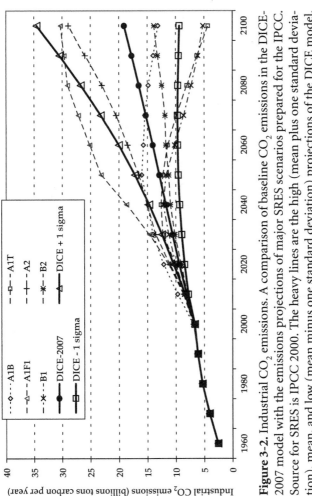

Figure 3-2. Industrial CO_2 emissions. A comparison of baseline CO_2 emissions in the DICE-2007 model with the emissions projections of major SRES scenarios prepared for the IPCC. Source for SRES is IPCC 2000. The heavy lines are the high (mean plus one standard deviation), mean, and low (mean minus one standard deviation) projections of the DICE model. The uncertainty range for the DICE-model projections is described in chapter 7. The range between the high (DICE +1 sigma) and low (DICE −1 sigma) projections is designed to capture 68 percent of the distribution of likely outcomes.

SOCIAL WELFARE FUNCTION

One of the major concerns about the earlier DICE model was their assumption of a relatively high pure rate of social time preference (3 percent per year). We note first, as discussed earlier, that the interpretation of the economic parameters is that they are designed to provide the most accurate projections rather than to be normative in nature. Additionally, the earlier assumptions were heavily influenced by numerical problems with alternative specifications and the requirement that the rate of return on capital be calibrated with observed market data.

In the revised version, we have lowered the pure rate of social time preference to 1.5 percent per year and have recalibrated the utility function to match market returns, yielding an elasticity of the marginal utility of consumption of 2. This revision moves the model closer to one that displays intergenerational neutrality while maintaining the calibration of the model's rate of return on capital with empirical estimates. Users should be aware that the sharp nonlinearity of the revised utility function may cause major scaling problems in computations and may therefore prove difficult to solve numerically; indeed, the unitary-elastic utility function was used in previous versions because we were unable to solve these computational problems in the earlier DICE models with higher elasticities.

DAMAGE FUNCTION

The basic structure of the regional damage functions follows the approach used in the RICE-1999 model. The major revisions involve recalibrating the costs of catastrophic damages, refining the estimates for regions with high temperature

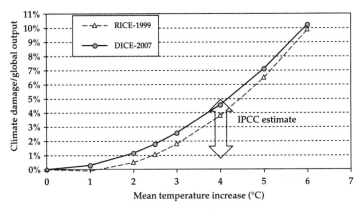

Figure 3-3. Damage function. The damage function used in the DICE-2007 model compared with the earlier study using the RICE-1999 model. The arrow shows the estimated range from IPCC 2007a, which reports that "global mean losses could be 1–5% GDP for 4°C of warming" (p. 20).

changes, and using revised estimates of the overall impacts for low damages. One result is that for small temperature changes, we estimate that there are positive damages, whereas in the 1999 model damages for small temperature changes were negative (that is, there were estimated positive net benefits). In addition, using PPP estimates of output results in a significantly higher world output; because damages are generally estimated as a fraction of output, total damages are also significantly higher in the 2007 model. The damage functions continue to be a major source of modeling uncertainty in the DICE model. Figure 3-3 shows the damage function contained in the DICE-2007 model compared with the earlier RICE model and the latest results from the IPCC Fourth Assessment Report (IPCC 2007a).

ABATEMENT-COST FUNCTION

The basic functional form for the abatement-cost function follows the structure assumed in the earlier DICE models. However, the structure has been reformulated over time to correct for an earlier modeling mistake. The implicit specification in the DICE model is that there is a "backstop technology." As noted earlier, this is a technology that can replace all carbon-emitting processes at a relatively high cost; that is, the backstop technology takes over when the emissions-control rate is 100 percent. The prior version used a functional form that implicitly and mistakenly assumed that the cost of the backstop technology increased over time.

The new version redefines the emissions-reduction equations by calibrating them to an explicit price and time profile of the backstop technology. The calibration of the new emissions-cost function is based on recent modeling efforts that calculate the cost of deep emissions cuts, the IPCC special report on sequestration (IPCC 2005), the IPCC Fourth Assessment Report, as well as modeling estimates provided by Jae Edmonds. In the new model, the cost of the backstop technology starts around $1,200 per metric ton of carbon and declines to $950 per metric ton by 2100.

The cost of the backstop technology appears high relative to other estimates, but it should be noted that this is the marginal cost of reducing the *last* unit of carbon emissions and not the cost for relatively inexpensive sources, such as coal-fired electricity generation. A substitute for fossil fuels such as nuclear power might be a backstop at $500 per ton of carbon replaced, but it might substitute only for electrical power. In other words, the $1,200 reflects the cost of replacing carbon from the last high-value use, such as plastics or jet fuel

or solvents. Although this new specification makes little difference in the short run (to the tactics of climate policy, so to
speak), it turns out that it makes a major difference over the
long run (to the strategy or vision).[10]

CARBON CYCLE

The new version of the DICE model does not change the basic
structure of the carbon-cycle model, but it recalibrates the initial stocks and the flow parameters. As noted earlier, the basic
strategy is to calibrate the DICE model to the MAGICC model,
primarily to the emissions scenarios that most closely resemble
those in the DICE projections, such as the A1F1 scenario.

     For reference purposes, we show in Table 3-1 a compar-
ison of the concentrations projections for the DICE model
with a model comparison from the Fourth Assessment Report of the IPCC. (This review became available after the
completion of the modeling design.) The table shows the
fraction of cumulative anthropogenic CO_2 concentrations
that are retained in the atmosphere by the IPCC models and
by the DICE model. For the historical period, the DICE
model is at the upper end of the models, with an atmospheric
retention ratio of 0.54, compared with 0.45 for the model en-
semble. For the total period, however, the DICE model has a
slightly lower atmospheric retention ratio of 0.51, versus 0.55
for the model mean. The major omission in the DICE model
is the absence of ocean carbonate chemistry that generates
lower ocean uptake over time in the more complete models.
It should be noted that the SRES scenario examined, A2, has
relatively flat emissions compared with the DICE-model
baseline.

Table 3-1. Comparison of Projections of Atmospheric CO$_2$ Retention Rate in DICE Model and IPCC Model

Model	Fraction of Cumulative Emissions Retained in Atmosphere	
	1850–2000	1850–2100
IPCC FAR		
Model mean	0.45	0.55
Range	0.43–0.61	0.45–0.72
DICE-2007	0.54	0.51

Note: These estimates in the DICE-2007 model and the IPCC Fourth Assessment Report (FAR) model show the fraction of total anthropogenic CO$_2$ emissions that were retained in the atmosphere for the periods 1850–2000 and 1850–2100. The emissions trajectories are not exactly comparable because the DICE model uses the baseline emissions, while the IPCC used the SRES scenario A2. Source for IPCC is IPCC 2007b, figure 7.13.

CLIMATE MODEL AND DATA

The basic structure of the climate model has not been significantly revised in the current DICE model. The timing has been changed to shorten the lag from radiative forcing to temperature change. The parameterization has been slightly revised, increasing the climate sensitivity from 2.9°C to 3.0°C per equilibrium CO$_2$-equivalent doubling, which is in line with the IPCC central estimate. In addition, the short-run adjustment parameters have been calibrated to fit the estimates from general circulation models and impulse-response experiments, particularly matching the forcing and temperature profiles in the MAGICC model. The estimates of non-CO$_2$ forcing and nonindustrial CO$_2$ emissions have been revised in light of recent estimates and the findings in the IPCC Third and Fourth Assessment Reports.

Figure 3-4 shows a comparison between the calibrated DICE model and the MAGICC model. For technical reasons, both are calibrated to a 2.6°C temperature-sensitivity parameter, but similar results hold for a 4.5°C temperature-sensitivity parameter. The DICE model has slightly lower projections for the same emissions path; over the twenty-first century the DICE-model structure projects a 3.61°C increase, while the MAGICC structure projects a 3.71°C increase.

INCOMPLETE PARTICIPATION

Earlier versions of the DICE model assumed that policies were harmonized among different regions and that all regions participated. The current version introduces a participation function. This allows model runs in which a subset of countries has emissions reductions (in a harmonized fashion), while the balance of countries undertakes no emissions reductions. Because of the functional form of the emissions equation in the DICE model, we can derive an exact mathematical representation of the result of incomplete participation. This new specification allows estimates, in the structure of an aggregate model, of the impact of alternative groupings of countries such as occurs in the Kyoto Protocol. We describe the participation structure and some results of incomplete participation in Chapter 6.

LIMITED FOSSIL-FUEL RESOURCES AND HOTELLING RENTS

Earlier versions of the DICE model focused on short-term projections and policies ("short-term" being up to 2100). In the current version, given the increased attention to long-term projections of climate, geophysical systems, and ecology, the

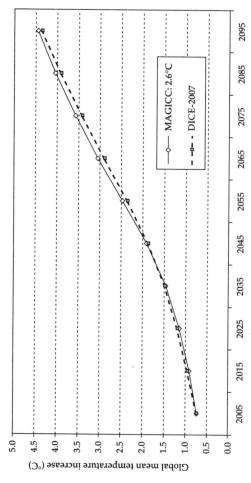

Figure 3-4. Comparison of temperature change. A comparison between the temperature profiles for the DICE-2007 model with a 2.6°C temperature sensitivity and the MAGICC programs with the same temperature sensitivity. The MAGICC runs are generated by the software at MAGICC 2007. The runs use the A1F1 CO_2 emissions and the radiative forcing for non-CO_2 greenhouse gases assumed in the MAGICC runs.

modeling has paid more attention to long-run consistency with major geophysical models and economic constraints. One major change has been to introduce long-run fossil-fuel availability constraints. In the new model, total resources of economically available fossil fuels are limited to 6,000 billion metric tons of carbon equivalent (approximately 900 years at current consumption rates). This constraint generates Hotelling rents that in the long run rise to drive consumption to the backstop technology. Although these constraints are unimportant in the base case for the short run (up to a century), they become important in cases of rapid economic growth or low rates of carbon-reducing technological change.

REAL RETURNS ON CAPITAL

One of the major economic variables for constructing a capital-based model is the real return on capital. We have constructed our model by using the Cobb-Douglas production function with explicit estimates of the capital stocks of different regions derived by the perpetual inventory method. As a check, we have compared the projections of the real return on capital in the DICE model with estimates of the real return from various studies. Table 3-2 shows the collation of the real returns on assets from the IPCC Second Assessment Report.[11] For the United States, the estimated returns are around 5 percent for most well-measured sectors, while numbers for other countries and sectors are sometimes much higher. In the DICE model, the estimated return on capital is between 5 and 6 percent per year for the first five decades. A further discussion of this question is contained in Chapter 9.

Table 3-2. Estimated Real Returns to Capital from IPCC Second Assessment, Various Periods and Sources

Asset	Period	Real Return (Percent)
High-income industrial countries		
Equities	1960–1984 (a)	5.4
Bonds	1960–1984 (a)	1.6
Nonresidential capital	1975–1990 (b)	15.1
Govt. short-term bonds	1960–1990 (c)	0.3
United States		
Equities	1925–1992 (a)	6.5
All private capital, pretax	1963–1985 (d)	5.7
Corporate capital, posttax	1963–1985 (e)	5.7
Real estate	1960–1984 (a)	5.5
Farmland	1947–1984 (a)	5.5
Treasury bills	1926–1986 (c)	0.3
Developing countries		
Primary education	various (f)	26
Higher education	various (f)	13

Source: Arrow et al. 1996. The letters refer to the sources provided in the background document.

Major Contentious Issues

Even though the DICE-2007 model is extremely simplified in many areas, it remains a complex nonlinear system with several contentious relationships. The model has 19 dynamic equations that contain 44 nontrivial parameters (omitting straightforward initial conditions such as world population, output, and global mean surface temperature anomaly). Some of these parameters are relatively inconsequential (such as the capital elasticity in the production function). Others are central (such as the temperature sensitivity for CO_2 doubling or the rate of growth of total factor productivity). Additionally, the structural equations are invariably aggregates of complicated nonlinear spatial and temporal relationships, and they are likely to be misspecified. In this section, I discuss three major issues that arise in all integrated assessment models of climate change and raise special issues in DICE-2007: the discount rate, uncertainty, and regionalization of the model.

THE DISCOUNT RATE

Controversies involving the discount rate have been central to global-warming models and policy for many years. These issues are discussed in detail in Chapter 9 on the *Stern Review*, and I will summarize the points briefly.

Some background on growth economics and discounting concepts is necessary to understand the issues about discounting. In choosing among alternative trajectories for emissions reductions, the key economic variable is the real return on capital, r, which measures the net yield on investments in capital, education, and technology. In principle, this is observable in the marketplace. For example, the real pretax return on U.S. corporate capital over the past four decades has averaged about 7 percent per year. Estimated real returns on human capital range from 6 to more than 20 percent per year, depending upon the country and time period (see Table 3-2). The return on capital is the discount rate that enters into the determination of the efficient balance between the cost of emissions reductions today and the benefit of reduced climate damages in the future. A high return on capital tilts the balance toward emissions reductions in the future, while a low return tilts reductions toward the present.

Where does the return on capital come from? Analyses of climate economics base the analysis of real returns on optimal economic growth theory. In this framework, the real return is an endogenous variable that depends upon two unobserved normative parameters. The first is the time discount rate, denoted by ρ. The time discount rate is a parameter that measures the importance of the welfare of future generations relative to the present. It is calculated in percentage per unit of time, like an interest rate, but refers to the discount in future "utility" or welfare, not future goods or dollars. A zero time discount rate means that future generations are treated symmetrically with present generations; a positive time discount rate means that the welfare of future generations is reduced or "discounted" compared with nearer generations.

The real return on capital also depends upon yet another unobserved normative parameter: the consumption elasticity, denoted by α. This parameter represents the aversion to inequality of different generations. A low (high) value of α implies that decisions take little (much) heed about whether the future is richer or poorer than the present. Under standard optimal growth theory, if time discounting is low and society cares little about inequality, then it will save a great deal for the future and the real return will be low. Alternatively, if either the time discount rate is high or society is averse to inequality, the current savings rate will be low and the real return will be high.

The basic economics can be described briefly. Assume a time discount rate of ρ and a consumption elasticity of α. Next, maximize the social welfare function described earlier and in the Appendix with a constant population and a constant rate of growth of consumption per generation, g^*. This yields the standard equation for the equilibrium real return on capital, r^*, given by $r^* = \rho + \alpha g^*$. This is the "Ramsey equation," which is the central organizing concept for thinking about intertemporal investment decisions and therefore about choices for global-warming policies. The Ramsey equation shows that in a welfare optimum, the rate of return on capital is determined by the time discount rate, the consumption elasticity, and the rate of growth of consumption. In a growing economy, a high return on capital can arise either from a high time discount rate or high aversion to intergenerational inequality.

The assumption behind the DICE model is that the time discount rate should be chosen along with the consumption elasticity so that the model generates a path that resembles the actual real interest rate. We have chosen a time discount rate of 1½ percent per year along with a consumption elasticity of 2. With this pair of assumptions, the real return on capital averages around 5½ percent per year for the first half century of the projections, and this is our estimate of the rate of return on capital. We could use alternative calibrations to get the same real returns; for example, these parameters could be modified to assume a time discount rate of 0.1 percent per year and a consumption elasticity of 2.9, and we would obtain the same real interest rate. Note as well that, unlike some economic models, the DICE model solves for the interest rate as a function of the underlying parameters rather than assuming the interest rate as an exogenous parameter. This approach allows changes in assumptions to be introduced easily.

There are important long-term implications of different combinations of time discount rates and consumption elasticities. However, the implications for near-term decisions (such as the optimal carbon tax, the optimal emissions-control rate, or the controls needed to limit GHG concentrations or temperature increases) are small as long as the real interest rate path starts along the same trajectory. The summary verdict is that the results over the near term of a half century or so are insensitive to the time discount rate (in the range of 0.1 to 3.0 percent per year) as long as the near-term trajectory of the real interest rate is maintained.

UNCERTAINTY

If global warming is the mother of all public goods, it may also be the father of decision making under uncertainty. In terms of model structure, every equation (except for the identities) contains major unresolved questions. Some of the important ones are, What will be the pace of world economic growth? What will be the damages in different regions, and how steep will those damages be if global warming proceeds beyond 2 or 3°C? How expensive will noncarbon backstop technologies prove to be? How difficult will it be to forge and sustain an international agreement on mitigation? How fast will developing countries move their labor forces and economies out of agriculture? What would be the economic benefit of a competitive, low-carbon energy source? There are major differences among scientists and economists on the answers to these questions, and it seems fair to conclude that there are unlikely to be definitive answers in the next few years. Moreover, we do not know how fast these uncertainties will be resolved, or what kinds of investments in learning would help resolve them.

The current version of the DICE model takes the first step of analyzing the economics of global warming under the assumption of perfect foresight or certainty equivalence.

(A certainty-equivalent approach calculates the model using the expected value of all the parameters.) This first step provides the basic intuition about the economics of alternative approaches. It also provides a first approximation to a complete answer under certain conditions (for example, where risk aversion is relatively low, functions are relatively linear, or risks are relatively small). Prior studies by the author and others provide inconsistent results about the impacts of uncertainty and learning on near-term policies (such as the control rate or the optimal carbon tax).[12]

A full treatment of uncertainty is beyond the scope of this book. We provide some preliminary results in Chapter 7 to give the flavor of the impacts of uncertainty. The tentative and surprising result of that analysis is that the certainty-equivalent policy is very close to the policy that is calculated using the expected-utility approach and a full range of uncertainties.

REGIONAL DISAGGREGATION

The DICE model is highly aggregated over time and space. The time-steps of 10 years collapse a great deal of time—for example, two Kyoto budget periods would fit into one time-step. Additionally, we have aggregated highly diverse regions from New York City to Mali into a grand global aggregate.

The aggregation is relatively unimportant for many parts of the integrated assessment model. For example, the regional distribution of GHG emissions is unimportant as long as the global total is correctly estimated. Moreover, if the geophysical equations are properly calibrated to accurate high-resolution models, then the global average results will be reasonably accurate as well. The major shortcoming of the globally aggregated approach is that it cannot calculate the costs and benefits of impacts and mitigation on individual regions and countries. It is also not possible to examine the effect of different coalitions, or of regionally differentiated policies, on the path of climate and economic activity.

The regional approach to the modeling is currently under way in a joint work with Zili Yang. The regional version of the model, known as the RICE or Regional Integrated model of Climate and the Economy, is planned for development and publication in 2008–2009. The regional model may also move to a shorter time-step (five years) to more closely match the budget period of the Kyoto Protocol.

IV
Alternative Policies for Global Warming

Summary

The major advantage of integrated assessment approaches such as the DICE model is that they can investigate alternative policies in a consistent and comprehensive framework. The costs and impacts of alternative policies on the environment and the economy can be analyzed as a package. This allows us to understand the trade-offs involved in a more precise fashion.

There are many potential approaches to climate-change policy. In this book, we have organized these into the major policies shown in Table 4-1. The first or baseline policy is a world in which there are no controls for two and one-half centuries. In this scenario, emissions are uncontrolled until 2250, after which a full set of controls is imposed. The next scenario is the economic optimum, in which the discounted value of utility is maximized. The next scenarios are ones in which there are limits on CO_2 concentrations or on global

Table 4-1. Alternative Policies Analyzed with the DICE-2007 Model

1. *No controls ("baseline").* No emissions controls for first 250 years.

2. *Optimal policy.* Emissions and carbon prices set at optimal levels from second period in 2010–2019.

3. *Climatic constraints with CO_2-concentration constraints.* Similar to optimal case except that CO_2 concentrations are constrained to be less than a given upper limit.

   A. CO_2 concentrations limited to 1.5 × preindustrial level (420 ppm)

   B. CO_2 concentrations limited to 2 × preindustrial level (560 ppm)

   C. CO_2 concentrations limited to 2.5 × preindustrial level (700 ppm)

4. *Climatic constraints with temperature constraints.* Similar to optimal case except that global temperature change is constrained to be less than a given increase from 1900.

   A. Temperature increase limited to 1.5°C

   B. Temperature increase limited to 2°C

   C. Temperature increase limited to 2.5°C

   D. Temperature increase limited to 3°C

5. *Kyoto Protocol.* These runs implement different variants of the Kyoto Protocol.

   A. *Original Protocol with the United States.* Implements the emissions limits of the Kyoto Protocol with constant emissions at level of 2008–2012 budget period including Annex I countries.

   B. *Original Kyoto Protocol without the United States.* Implements the emissions limits of the Kyoto Protocol with constant emissions at level of 2008–2012 budget period including Annex I countries except the United States.

   C. *Strengthened Kyoto Protocol.*

(continued)

Table 4-1. (continued)

---

6. *Ambitious proposals*
    A. *In the spirit of the* Stern Review: *Environmental discount rate.*
       This run uses the *Stern Review*'s real interest rate for climatic
       investments and the model's real rate for other investments.
    B. *Gore emissions reductions.* Achieve global emissions
       reductions of 90 percent by 2050.
7. *Low-cost backstop technology.* Development of a technology or
   energy source that can replace all fossil fuels at current costs.

---

temperature increases. Three scenarios investigate the implications of different versions of the Kyoto Protocol. One scenario investigates the costs of implementing controls implied
by the utility and discounting in the *Stern Review* (Stern 2007),
while another explores recent suggestions made by Al Gore.
The final scenario explores the economic benefit of a competitive, low-carbon energy source that can replace fossil fuels.

Detailed Description of Alternative Policies
NO CONTROLS ("BASELINE")

The first run is one in which no policies are taken to slow or
reverse greenhouse warming. Individuals and firms would
adapt to the changing climate, but governments are assumed
to take no steps to curb greenhouse-gas emissions or to inter-
nalize the greenhouse externality. This policy has been followed for the most part by nations through 2007, although
participants in the Kyoto Protocol will adopt binding constraints starting in 2008. The computational strategy here is
that the policy follows the market path for allocating carbon
fuels over time for 25 periods (250 years), after which the

world "wakes up" and optimizes its emissions trajectory in light of the damages of climate change.[1] We also show the results of a shorter delay period (50 years) for illustrative purposes.

"OPTIMAL" POLICY

The second case solves for an economically efficient or "optimal" policy to slow climate change. This can be interpreted as the economic optimum with no noneconomic constraints. (Note that the damages include nonmarket and catastrophic damages, but they exclude, for example, any "intrinsic value" of a given climate.) In this run, emissions are set to maximize the value of net economic consumption. More precisely, this run finds a trajectory for emissions reductions that balances current abatement costs against future damages from global warming. It assumes complete participation and compliance and is therefore extremely optimistic. It reduces emissions efficiently across regions and across time. The marginal costs of emissions reductions are always and everywhere equal to the marginal benefits of reducing emissions in terms of lower damages.

We should provide a word of caution about the optimal case. It is not presented in the belief that an environmental czar will suddenly appear to promulgate infallible canons of policy that will be religiously followed by all. Rather, the optimal policy is a benchmark to determine how efficient or inefficient alternative approaches may be. This is the best possible policy path for emissions reductions, given the economic, technological, and geophysical constraints that we have estimated. Note that the economic optimum places no intrinsic value on climate stability or other noneconomic or nonanthropocentric values. It does include an estimate of nonmarket damages from climate change, but these incorporate the costs of climate change only to the extent that they are of value to humans.

CLIMATIC CONSTRAINTS WITH CO_2-CONCENTRATION CONSTRAINTS

The next two sets of policy experiments impose climatic constraints on top of the economic costs and damages. The constraints considered here are concentrations limits (such as limiting CO_2 concentrations to two times the preindustrial level) or temperature constraints (such as limiting global temperature rise to 2°C from 1900 levels). These runs are similar to the optimal case except that the climatic constraints are imposed on top of the economic damage estimates. There are three subcases here:

A. CO_2 concentrations limited to 1.5 × preindustrial levels (420 ppm)
B. CO_2 concentrations limited to 2 × preindustrial levels (560 ppm)
C. CO_2 concentrations limited to 2.5 × preindustrial levels (700 ppm)

CLIMATIC CONSTRAINTS WITH TEMPERATURE CONSTRAINTS

Climatic constraints limiting temperature increase are similar to the optimal case except that global temperature change is constrained to be less than a given upper limit. There are four subcases here:

A. Temperature increase is limited to 1.5°C (from 1900 levels)

B. Temperature increase is limited to 2°C (from 1900 levels)

C. Temperature increase is limited to 2.5°C (from 1900 levels)

D. Temperature increase is limited to 3°C (from 1900 levels)

Binding constraints are difficult to rationalize from a purely economic point of view because it seems unlikely that there are limited costs up to a well-defined point and infinite costs after that. However, this idea is embodied in Article 2 of the United Nations Framework Convention on Climate Change, which declares its ultimate objective as "stabilization of greenhouse gas concentrations in the atmosphere at a level that would prevent dangerous anthropogenic interference with the climate system."[2]

The economic basis of a constraint based on dangerous interference might be that there are extremely costly thresholds, such as the disintegration of the West Antarctic Ice Sheet (WAIS) or the melting of the Greenland Ice Sheet (GIS).[3] Science suggests that these thresholds are not currently understood. For example, Oppenheimer and Alley (2004) suggest that we cannot judge whether the critical threshold for the melting of either the WAIS or the GIS is 1°C, 2°C, or 4°C of global warming or 10°C of local warming. We might set the threshold as the temperature limit where the probability of major sea-level rise increases sharply and exceeds some tolerable level. For example, it might be considered unacceptable to incur sufficient warming to melt the WAIS or the GIS. Another way to understand a threshold is to step outside the narrow confines of economic maximization and assume that we have a stewardship responsibility to future generations not to wreck the planet by triggering major sea-level rise, species extinction, or other ecological disruptions.

None of these arguments points to a specific threshold. There has been considerable analysis of the role of hard constraints and dangerous interferences, and we will not undertake an extensive analysis in this book.[4] Rather, the point here is to examine the trade-offs involved, particularly the incremental costs of imposing these climatic constraints in the context of abatement costs and climate damages in the DICE model. In other words, we ask how expensive it would be to add these threshold constraints to the economic optimum analyzed earlier. It is particularly useful and interesting from an economic perspective to examine the implications of different thresholds for near-term policy. With this objective in mind, we discuss our two sets of climatic targets, CO_2-concentration constraints and temperature constraints.

The first constrained runs stabilize the concentrations of CO_2 in the atmosphere. This policy is motivated by two ideas. First, the harmful impacts of climate change are produced by concentrations of GHG and then temperature and other climatic changes. Second, CO_2 concentrations are closely related to CO_2 emissions, which are in principle under the control of policy. As noted earlier, concentrations were specifically identified under the U.N. Framework Convention. Although no dangerous level has been established, some scientists believe that a prudent policy would be to limit atmospheric CO_2 concentrations to 560 ppm (two times their preindustrial levels). We take this policy along with a tighter and looser objective as our CO_2-concentration constraints. Note that this policy does not directly link to warming or temperature because it omits other radiative forcing and because of inertia and uncertainties about the concentration-temperature linkage.

An alternative and better-grounded objective involves taking steps to slow or stabilize the increase in global temperature. This approach is particularly interesting because it focuses on an objective that is closer to the area of actual concern (climate change) as opposed to most other policies, such as emissions or concentrations limits, which focus on intermediate variables of little or no intrinsic concern. The disadvantages of such a climatic objective are that it is less closely connected to actual policies and that the determinants of global temperature are poorly understood.

There have been a number of proposals for setting "tolerable windows" on climate change.[5] We take four cases that span a range from expensive but feasible (1.5°C) to one that is at the upper limit of what might be thought compatible with acceptable ecological damages and ice-sheet stability (3°C). (We do not examine higher temperature limits because they would not be binding for the optimal run and are therefore uninteresting to examine for the current model.)

In all the climatic targeting cases, we impose the constraint as a supplement to the economic cost-benefit optimization. The economic intuition of this approach is that the limit is interpreted as a threshold at which the damage function turns up sharply and damages become infinite. Although this economic interpretation should not be taken literally, it helps sharpen our understanding of the economic implications of potentially catastrophic climate change. Note also that these runs will differ from ones—call them "limits without damages"—that simply impose a climatic constraint (such as ones that limit CO_2 concentrations to 560 ppm). These approaches have been widely analyzed in the climate-change literature.[6] Although they are useful heuristic devices, imposing limits-without-damages constraints is economically flawed because it imposes the discontinuous cost threshold but ignores the climatic damages that are incurred before the threshold is reached. As a result, the limits-without-damages approach tends to have too-low emissions reductions at the beginning of the trajectory.

KYOTO PROTOCOL

We next study three variants of the Kyoto Protocol:

A. Original version extended indefinitely
B. Original version extended without the United States
C. Strengthened Kyoto Protocol

The current international regime for controlling greenhouse gases is the Kyoto Protocol. The original Protocol of 1997 was designed to limit the emissions of Annex I countries (essentially, Organization for Economic Cooperation and Development [OECD] countries plus Eastern Europe and most of the former Soviet Union). The Protocol states: "The Parties included in Annex I shall, individually or jointly, ensure that their aggregate anthropogenic carbon dioxide equivalent emissions of the greenhouse gases . . . do not exceed their assigned amounts, . . . with a view to reducing their overall emissions of such gases by at least 5 per cent below 1990 levels in the commitment period 2008 to 2012." The Protocol is scheduled to enter into force in 2008, with all major developed countries except the United States committing to keep their CO_2 emissions within the limits specified by the Protocol.

The analysis here is intended to be a broad-brush examination that allows a comparison of three variants of the Protocol with the other major approaches. All three variants assume that there is a group of countries that participates with an aggregate emissions-reduction target.[7] The analysis further assumes that the countries have complete harmonization of policies through emissions trading so that carbon prices are harmonized across participating regions. It allows no banking or borrowing, so there is no intertemporal price arbitrage. It further assumes that there are no emissions reductions in nonparticipating countries.

Under variant A, we examine the original Protocol with the original emissions limits extended indefinitely. Variant B is the same as A except that it excludes the United States from participation. These policies have been widely analyzed in the economic literature.[8] Variant C is more speculative and analyzes a deepened and broadened Protocol. The shortcomings of the existing version of the Kyoto Protocol are clear, and European countries and Japan have been advocating a stronger version. For example, in preparation for the 2007 G-8 Summit, Germany advocated a commitment to limit global warming to 2°C and a target reduction in global GHG emissions of 50 percent below 1990 levels by 2050. Although the Bush administration has rejected this proposal, future American administrations may engage in a similar effort.

The two parts of the German proposal are quite distinct. A policy with a temperature limit was discussed earlier. Our estimates indicate that the emissions target is tighter than would be necessary to attain a 2°C degree target, but that topic will be discussed later.

For an emissions-limitation approach, we analyze a "strengthened Kyoto Protocol." For this variant, we add countries gradually over the coming decades, and countries begin with 10 percent emissions reductions and then add further 10 percent emissions reductions every quarter century. Under this case, the United States enters the Protocol in 2015 and undertakes 50 percent emissions reductions by 2030; China enters in 2020 and has 50 percent emissions reductions by 2045; India is a decade behind China. Every region except sub-Saharan Africa is assumed to undertake significant emissions reductions by the middle of the twenty-first century. This strengthened approach yields a global emissions-reduction rate of 40 percent from the baseline in 2050, which is a global emissions level somewhat above 1990 levels and is less stringent than the German target just cited. If we look at the pace at which countries join and cut their emissions in the strengthened Kyoto Protocol, we may conclude that implementation would involve strenuous efforts virtually without precedent among international agreements.

In all Kyoto cases, we assume that the emissions reductions are efficiently undertaken, with the marginal cost of reductions (and the carbon price) equalized among all participating regions. All nonparticipating countries have unconstrained emissions and an implicit carbon price of zero.

"AMBITIOUS" PROPOSALS

The two approaches analyzed here are called "ambitious" in the sense that they call for very sharp emissions reductions in the near term. One of these is an estimate with a very low time discount rate and return on capital and is in the spirit of the analysis underlying the *Stern Review*. The other is motivated by a suggestion made by Al Gore for very deep near-term cuts in emissions.

In the Spirit of the Stern Review

As discussed earlier, one of the major controversies in studies of the economics of global warming has been the appropriate discount rate. To examine the role of discounting, one run has been undertaken with a near-zero discount rate and a unitary consumption elasticity. For this run, we adopted the time discount rate of 0.1 percent per year advocated by the *Stern Review*.[9] To implement this in a way that is comparable with other runs, we use a dual-discount-rate approach. Under this approach, we apply a very low real interest rate (around 1 percent per year) on climate investments, while the rest of the economy uses current discounting (at around 5.5 percent per year). This dual discounting is different from the approach in the *Stern Review,* in which the authors implicitly argue that the very low real interest rate applies universally rather than only in the climate sectors.

To model this run, we first optimize emissions reductions using the *Stern Review* objective function. This optimization produces very sharp emissions-reductions rates and carbon prices. We then rerun the DICE model with the standard discount rate and consumption elasticity but constrain the run to adopt the emissions reductions from that first stage. We then evaluate the costs and benefits using the standard discounting and economic assumptions used for other runs of the DICE model. As we will see, this approach leads to sharp initial emissions reductions because future damages are very lightly discounted. It leads to major inefficiencies because the low-return climatic investments induced by the low discount rate on climate investments crowd out high-return investments in nonclimate capital. We discuss the approach of the *Stern Review* in more detail in Chapter 9.

In the Spirit of the Gore Proposal

The final proposal is in the spirit of the one made by former Vice President Al Gore Jr. to Congress in March 2007. Although he made no concrete proposals in his written testimony, in his verbal testimony Gore proposed that U.S. emissions be reduced by 90 percent by 2050, along with other steps such as banning coal-fired plants and enhancing efficiency standards.[10] He later stated explicitly that the United States should "join an international treaty within the next two years that cuts global warming pollution by 90 percent in developed countries and by more than half worldwide in time for the next generation to inherit a healthy Earth."[11] To implement this proposal, it is assumed that the global emissions-control rate rises from 15 percent in 2010 to 90 percent in 2050. (These restrictions are actually less tight than a similar percentage reduction from a base year because of emissions rising uncontrolled.) Furthermore, it is assumed that the participation rate rises from an initial 50 percent to 100 percent by 2050. These are clearly ambitious targets, and it is useful to understand their economic and environmental implications.

A LOW-COST BACKSTOP TECHNOLOGY

A final scenario investigates the implications of developing a new energy source that could replace current fossil fuels in an environmentally benign way at costs that are competitive with today's technologies. This is labeled a "low-cost backstop." No such technology is currently available. Current estimates are that replacing substantially all fossil fuels would involve technologies with a marginal cost on the order of $1,000 per ton of carbon. However, over the longer run, there are many possible alternatives to fossil fuels, and we cannot rule out major innovations in noncarbon fuels over the next century and beyond. For example, nuclear-based hydrogen fuels have long been seen as a viable and sustainable long-run alternative.

Another possible but more problematic option would be technologies designed either to remove carbon from the atmosphere or to offset the climatic impacts of rising CO_2 concentrations. The latter of these, called geoengineering, involves large-scale climatic engineering to offset the warming effect of greenhouse gases. Geoengineering is at present the only economically competitive technology to offset global warming. The major geoengineering option is to inject particles into the upper atmosphere to increase the backscattering of sunlight and thereby cool the earth's surface. In essence, this would involve producing the climatic effect of several large volcanoes every year. A survey of this approach by a 1992 report of the U.S. National Academy of Sciences concluded, "Perhaps one of the surprises of this analysis is the relatively low costs at which some of the geoengineering options might be implemented."[12]

It should be emphasized that although several scientists have undertaken careful studies of geoengineering's impacts,[13] ecologists and climate scientists generally have grave reservations about its use for climatic modification. A particular concern is the increasing acidification of the oceans, which would not be reversed by approaches that change radiative forcing. Moreover, the climatic impacts of geoengineering have not been sufficiently studied and might actually lead to unanticipated results. Particularly worrisome is the fact that GHG accumulation and geoengineering represent two large interventions in the climate system, first raising and then lowering surface warming. Although the first-order effects might appear to cancel, there may be harmful unforeseen second-order effects.

For the present calculations, we analyze a generic new backstop technology but do not specify which of the alternatives it represents. For our calculations, we assume that the backstop has zero carbon content and replaces existing fossil fuels at a cost of $5 per metric ton of carbon. This number can be justified as the estimated cost of offsetting global warming by geoengineering technologies. It must be emphasized, however, that there is at present no environmentally benign technology that remotely approaches the assumed costs.

V
Results of the DICE-2007
Model Runs

We now describe the major result of the DICE-2007 model runs. At the outset, it must be emphasized that models such as DICE are primarily tools for understanding the behavior of complex systems. They are not truth machines. The results convey a spurious precision that does not accurately reflect the modeling, behavioral, and measurement errors and uncertainties. At the same time, integrated assessment models provide an essential discipline by ensuring that assumptions and conclusions are internally consistent and that the consequences of alternative assumptions or policies can be mapped out.

Overall Results

We first summarize the overall results for the alternative policies described in Chapter 4. Table 5-1 shows a summary of the different runs. The rows show the 16 different policies examined. The first two numerical columns show the net economic impact of different policies relative to the baseline policy. Recall that the baseline assumes no controls on greenhouse-gas emissions for the first 250 years. The column labeled "Objective Function" is the exact measure of the difference in the discounted value of utility relative to the baseline, using first-period consumption as the numéraire. In other words, it measures the present value of consumption under that policy minus the present value of consumption in the baseline (no-controls) case.

The second column is an approximation that measures the difference in the present value of damages and abatement. The two cost measures differ because of nonlinearities in the cost, damage, and utility functions. The next three columns show the present value of climate damages, the present value of abatement costs, and the sum of the abatement costs and damages. The sixth column shows the "social cost of carbon" in 2005, and the next two columns show the "carbon price" or "carbon tax" that is induced by the policy. The social cost of carbon refers to today; the carbon price refers to the first realistic period in which a global regime could be in place. Some discussion of the terminology is needed here. The social cost of carbon is the additional damage caused by an additional ton of carbon emissions. In a dynamic framework, it is the discounted value of the change in the utility of consumption denominated in terms of current consumption. The carbon price is the market price of carbon (say, in a trading regime) or the tax levied on carbon emissions (in a tax regime). The optimal carbon price, or optimal carbon tax, is the market price (or carbon tax) on carbon emissions that balances the incremental costs of reducing carbon emissions with the incremental benefits of reducing climate damages. In an uncontrolled regime, the social cost of carbon will exceed the (zero)

Table 5-1. Results of Major

Run	Difference from Base		Present-Value Climate Damages	Present-Value Abatement Costs
	Objective Function	Abatement Plus Damages		
	(Trillions of 2005 U.S. $)			
No controls				
250-year delay	0.00	0.00	22.55	0.04
50-year delay	2.34	2.14	18.85	1.60
Optimal	3.37	3.07	17.31	2.20
concentration limits				
Limit to $1.5 \times CO_2$	−14.87	−14.60	9.95	27.24
Limit to $2 \times CO_2$	2.88	2.67	15.97	3.95
Limit to $2.5 \times CO_2$	3.37	3.08	17.31	2.20
Temperature limits				
Limit to 1.5°C	−14.73	−14.44	9.95	27.08
Limit to 2°C	−1.60	−1.80	13.09	11.30
Limit to 2.5°C	2.27	1.99	15.32	5.28
Limit to 3°C	3.24	3.02	16.67	2.90
Kyoto Protocol				
Kyoto with United States	0.71	0.63	21.38	0.58
Kyoto w/o United States	0.15	0.10	22.43	0.07
Strengthened	1.00	0.71	16.01	5.87
Stern Review				
discounting	−16.95	−14.18	9.02	27.74
Gore proposal	−21.66	−21.36	10.05	33.90
Low-cost backstop	17.19	17.19	4.92	0.48

Note: The definitions of the different runs are provided in the text and in Table 4-1, as is an

Runs for DICE-2007 Model

Net Present-Value Abatement Costs Plus Climate Damages	Social Cost of Carbon	Carbon Tax		Global Temperature Change	
	2005	2010	2100	2100	2200
	(2005 U.S. $ per Ton of Carbon)			(°C from 1900)	
22.59	28.1	0.0	1.0	3.06	5.30
20.45	27.8	0.0	203.6	2.72	3.52
19.52	27.3	33.8	202.4	2.61	3.45
37.19	144.0	189.7	761.2	1.61	1.78
19.92	29.2	39.6	445.5	2.48	2.84
19.51	27.3	37.1	202.4	2.61	3.45
37.03	106.5	140.8	899.1	1.50	1.50
24.39	45.3	60.2	863.4	2.00	2.00
20.60	31.3	42.2	539.5	2.41	2.50
19.57	27.9	37.9	256.7	2.57	2.99
21.96	27.8	16.2	11.3	2.94	5.23
22.49	28.1	1.2	1.0	3.05	5.29
21.88	27.1	36.2	321.8	2.39	3.26
36.77	23.9	305.2	948.9	1.52	1.27
43.96	27.8	56.1	865.2	1.49	1.58
5.40	19.0	4.9	4.1	0.90	0.83

explanation of the different columns.

carbon price. In an optimal regime, the carbon tax will equal the social cost of carbon. The last two columns show the calculated global mean temperature change in 2100 and 2200 under the different policies.

We begin by examining the net economic gain of different policies relative to the baseline or no-controls policy. Figures 5-1 and 5-2 show the gains graphically. The optimal policy has a very substantial gain in net economic welfare totaling $3.4 trillion. Although this is a large absolute number, it is a small fraction, about 0.17 percent, of the discounted value of total future income.

The optimal policy does not differ significantly from policies that add a moderately tight climate limit to the economic cost-benefit optimum. Table 5-2 shows the incremental cost of adding a climate limit on top of the cost-benefit optimum. For all but the most stringent limits on concentrations or temperature increase, the cost of adding a climatic constraint on top of the cost-benefit optimum is quite small (in the order of $1 trillion or less). The policies of limiting temperature increases to 1.5 degrees or limiting CO_2 concentrations to 1.5 times preindustrial levels are extremely costly, given current technologies and realistic considerations about participation. The policy of limiting CO_2 concentrations to 2.5 times preindustrial levels is not binding, and so it is identical to the optimal run.

The interpretation of the results for climate limits is the following: The pure economic cost-benefit calculus indicates that a certain path of emissions reductions is economically beneficial. However, this path may omit other considerations, such as "stewardship" or risk aversion to concerns about moving outside tolerable windows of change. The calculations suggest that adding the climatic constraints—such as limiting CO_2 concentrations to two times their preindustrial levels or

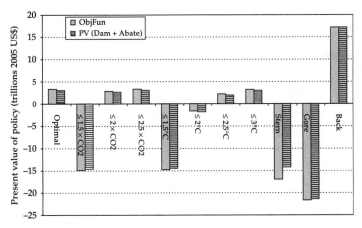

Figure 5-1. Present value of alternative policies. The difference in the present value of a policy relative to the baseline under two measures. The first bar is the value of the objective function in 2005 dollars (ObjFun), and the second is the present value of the sum of abatement and damages in the same units [PV (Dam +Abate)]. The policies are shown in Table 4-1. The baseline is omitted because it has zero present-value difference.

Legend for Chapter 5 figures: Optimal = optimal policy; ≤1.5 × CO_2 = CO_2 concentration limited to 1.5 times preindustrial level; ≤2 × CO_2 = CO_2 concentration limited to 2 times preindustrial level; ≤2.5 × CO_2 = CO_2 concentration limited to 2.5 times preindustrial level; ≤1.5°C = global temperature increase limited to 1.5°C; ≤2°C = global temperature increase limited to 2°C; ≤2.5°C = global temperature increase limited to 2.5°C; ≤3°C = global temperature increase limited to 3°C; Kyoto w U.S. = Kyoto Protocol with United States; Kyoto wo U.S. = Kyoto Protocol without United States; Strong Kyoto = Strengthened Kyoto Protocol; Stern = using the emissions controls induced by *Stern Review* discounting; Gore = proposal by Al Gore; Back = Low-cost backstop technology.

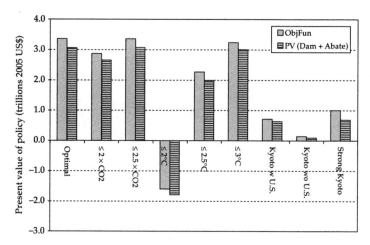

Figure 5-2. Present value of alternative policies. The same values as in Figure 5-1 with the larger values omitted for clarity. See Figure 5-1 for the definitions of policies.

limiting temperature change to 2.5°C—has a relatively low incremental price, as shown in Table 5-2. For those who believe that the economic approach misses important factors such as catastrophic risks or ecosystem values, these figures can be interpreted as the insurance premiums that would be required to add additional constraints to the cost-benefit calculus. In other words, the incremental costs are the net amount (abatement costs less averted damages) that would be required to keep the climate system within the prescribed limits.

The three Kyoto policies examined here are relatively inefficient and ineffective. The optimal policy reduces global temperature increase in 2200 by 2.1°C at an incremental abatement cost of $2.2 trillion (relative to the baseline). The current Kyoto policies have essentially no effect on global climate, while the

Table 5-2. Incremental Costs Imposed by Adding Climate Limits to Economic Optimum

Policy	Incremental Effect Relative to Optimal Policy		
	Present-Value Climate Damages	Present-Value Abatement Costs	Net Present-Value Costs Plus Damages
	(Trillions of 2005 U.S. Dollars)		
Limit to 1.5 × CO$_2$	−7.4	25.0	17.7
Limit to 2 × CO$_2$	−1.3	1.7	0.4
Limit to 2.5 × CO$_2$	0.0	0.0	0.0
Limit to 1.5°C	−7.4	24.9	17.5
Limit to 2°C	−4.2	9.1	4.9
Limit to 2.5°C	−2.0	3.1	1.1
Limit to 3°C	−0.6	0.7	0.0

strengthened Kyoto Protocol has an abatement cost 2.5 times the efficient policy's cost, with about the same effect on climate in 2200. These results confirm earlier modeling studies indicating that the Kyoto Protocol is highly cost-ineffective.[1]

The ambitious programs embedded in the *Stern Review* and Gore policies are extremely expensive. They succeed in reducing global temperature increases to between 1.3 and 1.6°C, but they do so at very high cost. The net cost of the ambitious proposals is between $17 trillion and $22 trillion relative to the baseline and between $20 trillion and $25 trillion relative to the optimum. The inefficiency of these approaches is due to the fact that they involve emissions reductions that are too sharp and too early in time and therefore do not allow for intertemporal efficiency.

The low-cost backstop scenario assumes the existence of an energy source that is environmentally safe and competitive with fossil fuels. This option is extremely attractive from an economic vantage point, with a positive present value of $17 trillion relative to the baseline. Although it might not be currently feasible, the high value of the low-cost backstop technology suggests that intensive research on such energy sources is justified.

Table 5-3 shows the incremental costs, damages, and benefit-cost ratio for each of the different policies. As shown in Table 5-1, the sum of the abatement costs and damages is slightly different from the net economic effect because of nonlinearities, but the sum of the abatement and damage costs provides a good approximation of the economic impacts. Any policy with a benefit-cost ratio below 1 has negative net economic value relative to no controls. Most of the policies pass a benefit-cost test relative to the baseline. The exceptions—the worse-than-nothing cases—are the Stern proposal, the Gore proposal, and very tight controls (such as extremely tight temperature or CO_2 limits).

In judging these ratios, recall that policies are assumed to have complete participation and to be efficiently implemented. If inefficient implementation occurs (say, through inefficient allocation of permits, differential standards, exclusions, inefficient taxation, or regional exemptions), then the costs will rise and the benefit-cost ratio of even the optimal policy could easily decline below 1.

Table 5-3 also shows the impact of different proposals on costs and damages separately. There are clearly big stakes involved in climate-change policies. Efficient policies can avoid at least $5 trillion in discounted damages with costs of less than half that. On the other hand, inefficient programs can

**Table 5-3. Incremental Abatement Costs and Damages
Relative to Baseline, and Benefit-Cost Ratio
of Different Approaches**

Policy	Benefits (Reduced Damages)	Abatement Costs	Benefit-Cost Ratio
	(Trillions of 2005 U.S. $)		
50-year delay	3.69	1.55	2.4
Optimal	5.23	2.16	2.4
Concentration limits			
Limit to 1.5 × CO_2	12.60	27.20	0.5
Limit to 2 × CO_2	6.57	3.90	1.7
Limit to 2.5 × CO_2	5.24	2.16	2.4
Temperature limits			
Limit to 1.5°C	12.60	27.03	0.5
Limit to 2°C	9.45	11.25	0.8
Limit to 2.5°C	7.22	5.24	1.4
Limit to 3°C	5.88	2.86	2.1
Kyoto Protocol			
Kyoto with United States	1.17	0.54	2.2
Kyoto w/o United States	0.12	0.02	5.0
Strengthened	6.54	5.82	1.1
Stern Review *discounting*	13.53	27.70	0.5
Gore proposal	12.50	33.86	0.4
Low-cost backstop	17.63	0.44	39.9

Note: The numbers are differences from the baseline case of no controls.

easily cost $5 trillion, $10 trillion, or $30 trillion more than efficient programs. We will examine the patterns of inefficiency later.

We also calculate the incremental abatement costs and climate damages as a percentage of income in Figure 5-3 (all

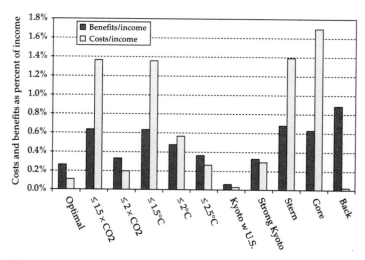

Figure 5-3. Costs and benefits as percentage of income. Abatement costs and benefits (reduced damages) for major policies are separated and shown as a percentage of total income (all figures are discounted at the consumption discount rate). Figures are shown relative to the baseline of no controls. See Figure 5-1 for the definitions of polices.

discounted values). For moderately efficient policies, the abatement cost is limited to between 0.1 and 0.25 percent of income (on a present-value basis). This is much less than the costs under the ambitious programs implicit in the Stern and Gore proposals, in which abatement costs amount to around 1.5 percent of income (the *Stern Review* estimates the present value of abatement costs to be 1 percent of income). Averted damages are substantial because our estimates of the potential damages of climate change are large. Efficient policies reduce damages by 0.2 to 0.4 percent of global income, while the most stringent policies reduce damages by at most 0.6 percent of income.

Emissions Controls, the Social Cost of Carbon, and Carbon Prices

One of the most important calculations in the DICE model is the social cost of carbon (SCC). Our estimate, shown in Table 5-1, is that the SCC with no interventions is about $28 per metric ton of carbon in 2005. This result is slightly below the average reported in the IPCC Fourth Assessment Report.[2] The SCC is always at or above the optimal carbon tax, but in our calculations the difference is relatively small in early periods.

The SCC in the baseline case is particularly informative because it indicates the maximum value that any efficient emissions-control program should take. In other words, a partial program (such as one with less than complete participation) might have a carbon price above the optimal carbon price, but never above the SCC. Note also that the SCC is well below the carbon price in approaches that impose inefficiently tight controls, such as the *Stern Review* and the Gore proposal.

Table 5-4 and Figure 5-4 show the carbon prices associated with the different policies. For most cases analyzed here, the prices are assumed to be harmonized within and among countries. Harmonization could occur either through harmonized taxes or through a system of fully tradable emissions permits.

The optimal policy has a carbon tax of $34 per metric ton of carbon in 2010 (all calculations are in 2005 international U.S. dollars).[3] The optimal tax rises in future years, reaching $42 per ton in 2015, $90 per ton in 2050, and $202 per ton in 2100. For reference, a carbon tax of $20 per metric ton would raise coal prices by $10 per ton, which is about 40 percent of the current U.S. mine-mouth coal price in 2005.

Table 5-4. Carbon Prices or Taxes for Different Policies

Policy	2005	2015	2025	2035	2045	2055	2065	2075	2085	2095	2105
				(2005 U.S. Dollars per Ton of Carbon)							
No controls											
250-year delay	0.08	0.03	0.04	0.07	0.10	0.15	0.23	0.35	0.53	0.79	1.18
50-year delay	0.08	0.03	0.04	0.07	0.10	99.31	118.26	139.33	162.82	189.02	218.25
Optimal	27.28	41.90	53.39	66.49	81.31	98.01	116.78	137.82	161.37	187.68	217.02
concentration limits											
Limit to 1.5 $\times CO_2$	144.04	247.61	421.92	609.52	659.23	695.10	720.73	738.71	750.96	758.88	763.51
Limit to 2 $\times CO_2$	29.24	45.11	58.67	75.18	95.69	121.96	157.06	206.45	280.13	396.87	494.11
Limit to 2.5 $\times CO_2$	27.28	41.90	53.39	66.49	81.31	98.01	116.78	137.82	161.37	187.68	217.02
Temperature limits											
Limit to 1.5°C	106.50	174.68	268.94	410.07	611.49	870.32	1,018.38	997.24	818.69	932.67	865.51
Limit to 2°C	45.30	71.82	102.25	146.01	209.83	303.07	436.46	615.52	817.77	919.77	807.01

Limit to 2.5°C	31.29	48.48	64.04	83.72	109.15	142.90	188.88	252.76	341.91	463.38	615.68
Limit to 3°C	27.89	42.89	54.98	69.04	85.38	104.52	127.16	154.40	187.82	229.76	283.55
Kyoto Protocol											
Kyoto with United States	0.08	15.02	15.72	14.74	13.70	12.95	12.40	11.99	11.67	11.43	11.25
Kyoto w/o United States	0.08	1.56	1.08	0.95	0.93	0.95	0.23	0.35	0.53	0.79	1.18
Strengthened	0.08	19.82	53.15	114.51	181.34	223.05	251.54	275.48	296.34	314.21	329.30
Stern Review											
discounting	248.98	336.38	408.68	480.24	554.59	633.89	719.59	812.89	915.08	958.01	939.82
Gore proposal	24.99	94.14	264.73	501.28	794.11	948.82	928.56	909.29	890.96	873.52	856.93
Low-cost backstop	5.00	4.88	4.76	4.65	4.55	4.45	4.35	4.26	4.18	4.09	4.02

Note: Prices are globally averaged. For most cases, carbon prices are harmonized across regions through trading or uniform taxes. Note that first-period prices begin in 2008 at the earliest and represent the impact of the Kyoto Protocol.

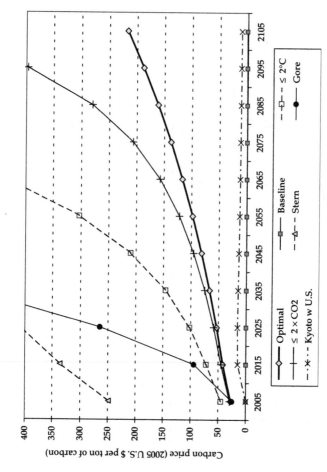

Figure 5-4. Carbon prices under different policies. The globally averaged carbon price under different policies over the next century. Note the upward tilt of the strategies. These prices are per ton of carbon; for prices per ton of CO_2, divide by 3.67.

Further, a carbon tax of $10 per ton would raise gasoline prices by about 4 U.S. cents per gallon.

The no-controls case has an initial Hotelling rent of $0.07 per ton of carbon (reflecting the relative abundance of carbon fuels). Policies that stabilize CO_2 concentrations and temperature have initial carbon taxes close to those in the optimal policy for all but the tightest targets. These taxes tend to rise sharply as the target approaches, as is seen particularly for the tight concentration and temperature targets. The optimal policy to meet these targets delays high carbon taxes to the future. Reducing future emissions is a cost-effective way to meet economic and climatic targets both because it is less expensive in a present-value sense and because some of the current emissions will have been removed from the atmosphere when the target becomes a binding constraint.

Table 5-5 and Figure 5-5 show the emissions-control rate for CO_2 in the different policies. These show the extent to which GHG emissions are reduced below their reference levels. In the optimal path, emissions reduction begins at a rate of about 16 percent of baseline emissions in the second model period (2011–2020) and climbs slowly over the next century, reaching about 25 percent by 2050. The tightest climate-target paths start with relatively low emissions-control rates but then climb sharply to emissions-control rates between 25 and 80 percent by midcentury. (Interpretation of the first period, 2000–2009, is complicated because most of that period is history. We assume that policies are introduced in 2011 unless otherwise stated.)

The economic problems with the ambitious Gore and Stern strategies are shown by the high emissions-control rates and carbon prices that they prescribe. The 80 to 90 percent control rates by the mid-twenty-first century require (according to our estimates) carbon prices in the range of $600

Table 5-5. Emissions-Control Rates for Different Policies

Policy	2005	2015	2025	2035	2045	2055	2065	2075	2085	2095	2105
					(Fraction of Global Baseline Emissions)						
No controls											
250-year delay	0.005	0.003	0.003	0.005	0.006	0.007	0.009	0.012	0.015	0.019	0.024
50-year delay	0.005	0.003	0.003	0.005	0.006	0.271	0.302	0.335	0.370	0.406	0.444
Optimal	0.005	0.159	0.185	0.212	0.240	0.269	0.300	0.333	0.368	0.404	0.443
concentration limits											
Limit to $1.5 \times CO_2$	0.005	0.428	0.583	0.725	0.766	0.799	0.825	0.846	0.864	0.879	0.891
Limit to $2 \times CO_2$	0.005	0.166	0.195	0.227	0.262	0.304	0.354	0.417	0.500	0.613	0.700
Limit to $2.5 \times CO_2$	0.005	0.159	0.185	0.212	0.240	0.269	0.300	0.333	0.368	0.404	0.443
Temperature limits											
Limit to 1.5°C	0.005	0.352	0.454	0.581	0.735	0.905	1.000	1.000	0.906	0.985	0.955
Limit to 2°C	0.005	0.215	0.265	0.328	0.406	0.504	0.625	0.765	0.906	0.978	0.919

Limit to 2.5°C	0.005	0.173	0.205	0.240	0.282	0.332	0.392	0.466	0.558	0.668	0.791
Limit to 3°C	0.005	0.162	0.188	0.216	0.246	0.279	0.315	0.355	0.400	0.452	0.514
Kyoto Protocol											
Kyoto with United States	0.005	0.090	0.094	0.092	0.089	0.087	0.086	0.086	0.085	0.085	0.086
Kyoto w/o United States	0.005	0.026	0.021	0.020	0.020	0.020	0.009	0.012	0.015	0.019	0.024
Strengthened	0.005	0.105	0.184	0.286	0.374	0.425	0.460	0.489	0.515	0.538	0.556
Stern Review discounting	0.423	0.507	0.573	0.635	0.696	0.759	0.825	0.893	0.964	1.000	1.000
Gore proposal	0.005	0.250	0.450	0.650	0.850	0.950	0.950	0.950	0.950	0.950	0.950
Low-cost backstop	1.000	1.000	1.000	1.000	1.000	1.000	1.000	1.000	1.000	1.000	1.000

Note: The emissions-control rates for the first period begin in 2008 unless otherwise stated. These control rates are beyond any "negative cost" abatement.

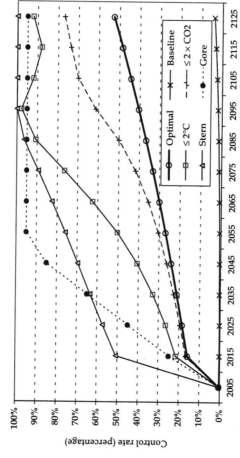

Figure 5-5. Emissions-control rates under different policies. The global emissions-control rate for CO_2 under different policies over the next century. Note the upward-tilted ramp of the strategies.

to $900 per ton of carbon. The dislocations involved in these prices are extremely large, and the economic costs are consequently also large. These carbon price estimates also apply to the recent German proposal for a 50 percent cut in global emissions from 1990 levels by the mid-twenty-first century.

Emissions, Concentrations, and Climate Change

EMISSIONS

We next examine the impact of different policies on the climatic variables. Table 5-6 and Figure 5-6 show the aggregate industrial CO_2 emissions per decade. Projections of baseline or uncontrolled industrial CO_2 emissions in DICE-2007 continue to rise rapidly in coming decades, reaching 19 billion tons of carbon (gigatons of carbon, or GtC) annually in 2100. In the optimal case, emissions are limited to 12.5 GtC annually in 2100.

Annual emissions follow a hump-shaped pattern for the scenarios with emissions reductions, with the hump being around 2100 for the optimal case and around 2050 for the climate restrictions. None of the efficient paths—even the one restricting the temperature increase to 2°C—calls for declining emissions paths from the start. By comparison, the ambitious programs of Gore and Stern call for immediate emissions reductions or limitations. The front-loaded emissions reductions in the ambitious proposals lead to much more costly profiles than the ones that are efficiently constructed and hump shaped.

CONCENTRATIONS

Atmospheric concentrations of CO_2 are shown in Table 5-7 and Figure 5-7. Beginning at an atmospheric concentration of

Table 5-6. Global Emissions of Industrial CO_2 per Decade by Policy

Policy	2005	2015	2025	2035	2045	2055	2065	2075	2085	2095	2105
				(Billions of Metric Tons of Carbon per Decade, Industrial Sources)							
No controls											
250-year delay	74.3	87.4	99.7	111.5	123.1	134.7	146.5	158.6	171.1	184.1	197.5
50-year delay	74.3	87.5	99.7	111.5	123.1	99.0	103.3	106.8	109.7.	111.7	112.8
Optimal	74.3	73.7	81.6	88.3	94.2	99.3	103.6	107.2	110.1	112.1	113.1
Concentration limits											
Limit to 1.5 × CO_2	74.3	50.1	41.6	30.7	28.7	27.0	25.6	24.5	23.5	22.7	22.0
Limit to 2 × CO_2	74.3	73.1	80.6	86.6	91.4	94.5	95.6	93.7	87.0	72.8	60.9
Limit to 2.5 × CO_2	74.3	73.7	81.6	88.3	94.2	99.3	103.6	107.2	110.1	112.1	113.1
Temperature limits											
Limit to 1.5°C	74.3	56.7	54.5	46.8	32.7	12.8	0.0	0.0	16.1	2.8	9.0
Limit to 2°C	74.3	68.8	73.4	75.2	73.5	67.2	55.5	37.7	16.4	4.2	16.4

Limit to 2.5°C	74.3	72.5	79.6	85.1	88.9	90.7	89.9	85.7	76.9	62.4	42.5
Limit to 3°C	74.3	73.5	81.3	87.8	93.4	97.9	101.4	103.7	104.4	103.0	98.7
Kyoto Protocol											
Kyoto with United States	74.3	79.8	90.7	101.7	112.8	123.9	135.2	146.8	159.0	171.8	185.3
Kyoto w/o United States	74.3	85.4	97.9	109.8	121.3	132.9	146.5	158.6	171.7	184.1	197.5
Strengthened	74.3	78.5	81.6	80.0	77.6	78.1	80.0	82.0	84.3	86.8	89.6
Stern Review	43.1	43.2	42.7	40.9	37.6	32.7	25.9	17.2	6.2	0.0	0.0
discounting											
Gore proposal	74.3	65.9	55.2	39.3	18.6	6.8	7.3	8.0	8.6	9.3	10.1
Low-cost backstop	0.0	0.0	0.0	0.0	0.0	0.0	0.0	0.0	0.0	0.0	0.0

Note: Policies are assumed to be introduced in 2008 unless otherwise stated.

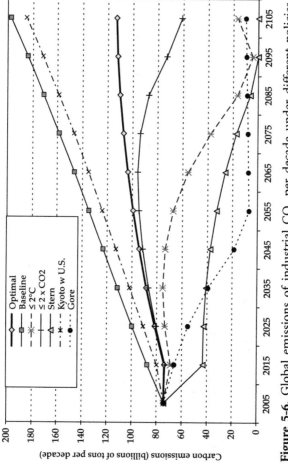

Figure 5-6. Global emissions of industrial CO$_2$ per decade under different policies. The global emissions of industrial CO$_2$ under different policies over the next century. The figure for 2005 is the actual value.

Table 5-7. Atmospheric CO$_2$ Concentrations by Policy

Policy	2005	2015	2025	2050	2100	2200
	(Atmospheric Concentrations, Parts per Million of Carbon)					
No controls						
250-year delay	379.8	405.2	432.7	507.9	685.9	1,182.6
50-year delay	379.8	405.2	432.7	507.9	602.9	667.6
Optimal	379.8	405.2	426.2	480.9	586.4	658.5
Concentration limits						
Limit to 1.5 ×CO$_2$	379.8	405.2	415.1	420.2	420.2	420.2
Limit to 2 ×CO$_2$	379.8	405.2	425.9	479.0	557.8	558.0
Limit to 2.5 ×CO$_2$	379.8	405.2	426.2	480.9	586.4	658.5
Temperature limits						
Limit to 1.5°C	379.8	405.2	418.2	434.4	400.4	388.2
Limit to 2°C	379.8	405.2	423.9	466.2	464.9	442.2
Limit to 2.5°C	379.8	405.2	425.7	477.3	544.4	504.6
Limit to 3°C	379.8	405.2	426.1	480.4	579.3	575.7
Kyoto Protocol						
Kyoto with United States	379.8	405.2	429.1	496.0	660.3	1,166.2
Kyoto w/o United States	379.8	405.2	431.7	505.6	684.0	1,181.5
Strengthened	379.8	405.2	428.5	474.9	543.8	629.2
Stern Review *discounting*	379.8	390.5	400.0	417.0	404.4	361.2
Gore proposal	379.8	405.2	422.5	430.9	399.2	399.4
Low-cost backstop	379.8	370.3	363.3	352.2	340.3	325.2

380 ppm in 2005, baseline concentrations rise to 686 ppm in 2100 and 1,183 ppm in 2200. In the optimal control case, concentrations are limited to 586 ppm in 2100 and 659 ppm in 2200. Most of the differences between the CO$_2$ concentrations in the economic optimum and in the climatic-limits cases come after 2050.

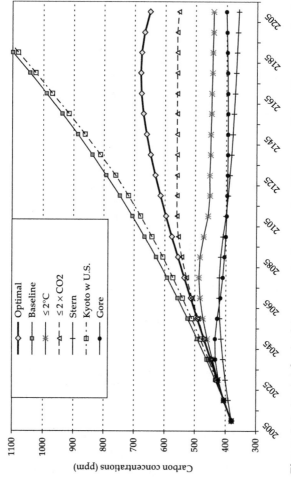

Figure 5-7. Atmospheric CO_2 concentrations under different policies. The atmospheric concentrations of CO_2 under different policies over the next century. The figure for 2005 is the actual value.

TEMPERATURE INCREASE

The increases in global mean temperature are shown in Table 5-8 and Figure 5-8. The baseline temperature increase of 0.73°C in 2005 (relative to the 1890–1910 average). The projected increase for the baseline scenario is 3.06°C by 2100 and 5.30°C by 2200. Clearly, according to the DICE-model projections, major warming is in store because of past emissions and climatic inertia. By comparison, the economic optimum has a projected increase of 2.61°C by 2100 and 3.45°C by 2200.

Except for the ambitious policy proposals of Gore and Stern, all runs have very similar concentration and temperature trajectories through the middle of the twenty-first century. After 2050, the scenarios with economic or climatic limits begin to trend downward relative to the other paths. The ambitious programs show a much sharper downward tilt, with warming for both cases peaking at around 1.6°C. The most successful emissions limitation is, of course, the low-cost backstop technology, which has zero effective emissions. Even with zero future emissions, however, the global temperature increase is close to 1°C.

One of the sobering results of integrated assessment analyses shown in these figures is how difficult it is to have a major impact on the temperature trajectory over the next century because of inertia in the economic and climate systems. The optimal path reduces global mean temperature by about 0.5°C relative to the baseline in 2100. Even if emissions were reduced 50 percent relative to the baseline by the mid-twenty-first century, global temperature change would still be at least 2°C. Only the ambitious paths, with excess abatement costs of $25 trillion to $34 trillion in present value (1.2 to 1.7 percent of global output), make a very large dent in global warming by

Table 5-8. Projected Global Mean Temperature Change by Policy

Policy	2005	2015	2025	2050	2100	2200
	(Temperature Increase from 1900, Degrees C)					
No controls						
250-year delay	0.73	0.96	1.20	1.82	3.06	5.30
50-year delay	0.73	0.96	1.20	1.81	2.72	3.52
Optimal	0.73	0.95	1.17	1.68	2.61	3.45
Concentration limits						
Limit to 1.5 × CO_2	0.73	0.94	1.10	1.36	1.61	1.78
Limit to 2 × CO_2	0.73	0.95	1.16	1.67	2.48	2.84
Limit to 2.5 × CO_2	0.73	0.95	1.17	1.68	2.61	3.45
Temperature limits						
Limit to 1.5°C	0.73	0.94	1.12	1.43	1.50	1.50
Limit to 2°C	0.73	0.95	1.15	1.61	2.00	2.00
Limit to 2.5°C	0.73	0.95	1.16	1.66	2.41	2.50
Limit to 3°C	0.73	0.95	1.17	1.68	2.57	2.99
Kyoto Protocol						
Kyoto with United States	0.73	0.96	1.18	1.76	2.94	5.23
Kyoto w/o United States	0.73	0.96	1.20	1.81	3.05	5.29
Strengthened	0.73	0.95	1.17	1.66	2.39	3.26
Stern Review *discounting*	0.73	0.89	1.03	1.31	1.52	1.27
Gore proposal	0.73	0.95	1.14	1.42	1.49	1.58
Low-cost backstop	0.73	0.80	0.84	0.86	0.90	0.83

Note: Increases are relative to the 1900 average.

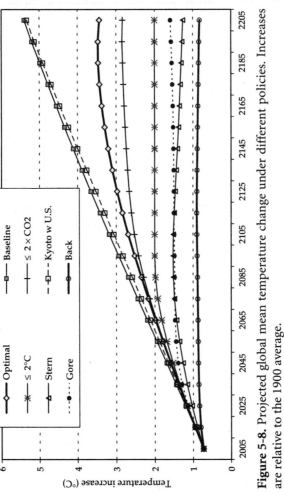

Figure 5-8. Projected global mean temperature change under different policies. Increases are relative to the 1900 average.

2100. However, the efficient policies have a more substantial impact over the longer run. Relative to the baseline, the temperature reductions in 2200 of the optimal path, the CO_2-concentration-doubling target, and the 2.5°C temperature target are 1.85, 2.46, and 2.80°C, respectively.

Other Economic Variables

The model includes many other economic and environmental variables that are part of the integrated assessment analysis. Figure 5-9 shows per capita consumption for a representative set of scenarios, while Figure 5-10 shows the historical and projected carbon-output ratio.

Two points about the trends should be noted. First, the model assumes continued rapid economic growth in the years ahead, although with slightly slower growth than over the past four decades. The average growth in global per capita consumption (PPP weighted across countries) over the 1960–2000 period was around 2.5 percent per year. The DICE-model projection for the 2000–2100 period is 1.3 percent per year. This leads to a level of per capita consumption of $25,000 in 2105, compared with $6,620 in 2005. This growth will lead to increased emissions, but it will also improve living standards and provide resources for coping with global warming.

A second feature of the DICE-2007 projection is a projected slowing in the rate of decarbonization in the baseline projection, shown in Figure 5-10. Over the 1965–2005 period, the estimated decline in the CO_2-GDP ratio was 1.7 percent per year. However, our disaggregated projections envision both less of a shift to low-carbon fuels and more of a rise in the share of developing countries with high CO_2-GDP ratios (such as China). These trends together imply that the decline in the

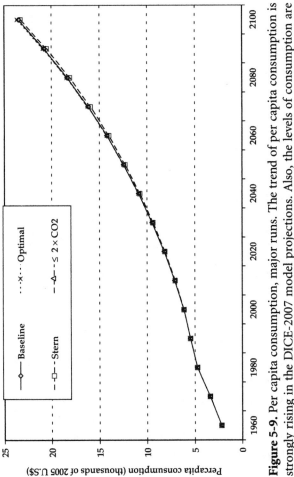

Figure 5-9. Per capita consumption, major runs. The trend of per capita consumption is strongly rising in the DICE-2007 model projections. Also, the levels of consumption are virtually indistinguishable among the different policies.

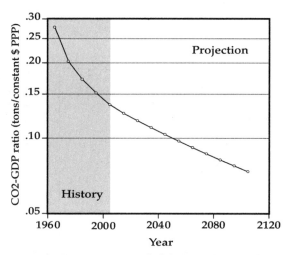

Figure 5-10. Carbon intensity of global production, history and projection, 1965–2105. The history and DICE-model projections of the carbon intensity of production, which is defined as CO_2 emissions per constant-price unit of world output. Because this is a logarithmic scale, the slope is the average growth rate. Note that the rate of decarbonization (as measured by the negative growth rate) has slowed in recent years.

CO_2-GDP ratio over the next century will be only 0.6 percent per year. This trend has important implications for the Kyoto Protocol because the Kyoto Protocol constrains only high-income countries. It also means that a substantial part of the "free" decarbonization that we have enjoyed over the past half century may not be available in the next few years.

Additionally, we emphasize that the size of the income redistribution under some of the policies is substantial. Figure 5-11 shows the carbon revenue transfers as a percentage of total consumption for different policies and periods. The revenue transfers are the total dollars transferred from consumers

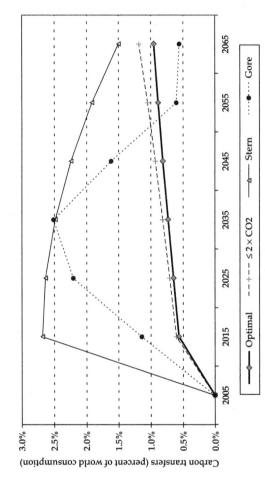

Figure 5-11. Carbon revenue transfers as a percentage of world consumption. The total transfers from consumers to producers and taxpayers due to carbon restrictions. These would apply whether the restrictions were imposed by cap-and-trade measures or by carbon taxes. The transfers are carbon prices times carbon use, while the denominator of the fraction is world consumption expenditures.

to producers (if permits are allocated to producers) or to governments (if constraints are imposed through efficient carbon taxes). The redistribution of income is a substantial fraction of world consumption, particularly for the ambitious plans. We put these numbers in perspective in the final chapter of this book.

Why Have the Estimated Optimal Carbon Taxes Increased since 1999?

The current round of DICE modeling provides estimates of the optimal carbon tax that are much larger than those in the last round. In the RICE/DICE model of 1999, the optimal carbon tax was estimated to be $9.13 per ton of carbon in 2005, whereas in the current round the estimate is $27.28 per ton of carbon. What accounts for this large difference?

There have been many changes in the model structure and data since the last complete round, as described in earlier chapters. It would be very tedious to go through the impact of every change. Rather, we can take a shortcut by making a very simple approximation of the optimal carbon tax. Under highly simplified assumptions, the optimal carbon tax is proportional to $(Z \times TSC \times Y) / R$, where Z is the ratio of damages to output at 3°C, TSC is the temperature-sensitivity coefficient, Y is world output, and R is the average discount factor.[4]

Table 5-9 shows a decomposition of the increase in the nominal value of the optimal carbon tax into the major factors. We have shown the changes as logarithmic percentages, which are the differences between the natural logarithms of two numbers in percentage terms. The logarithmic percentage is the same as the usual percentage change for small numbers. It has the advantage of being additive, unlike the usual

Table 5-9. Comparison of Major Assumptions and Results for DICE-2007 and DICE-1999

	Variable	DICE/RICE-1999	DICE-2007	Percentage Difference*
a	World GDP, 2005 (trillions of U.S. $)	30.52	55.58	60
	Components of GDP change:			
	a1 Inflation			32
	a2 Change from MER to PPP			29
	a3 Projection errors plus composition effects			−1
b	Change in damage function			64
c	Change in real interest rate			−27
d	Temperature-sensitivity coefficient	2.90	3.00	3
e	Sum of factors			100
f	Carbon tax, 2005 ($ per ton of carbon)	9.13	27.28	109

Note: Major determinants of the carbon taxes in the DICE-2007 model with the comparable estimate in the DICE/RICE-1999 model.

*The percentage differences are in natural logarithms. Therefore, the difference between 1 and 1.1 = ln(1.1) = 0.095 = 9.5 percent, while the difference between 1 and 2 = ln(2) = 0.693 = 69.3 percent. The advantage of using logarithmic percentages is that the sum of the different factors adds exactly to the total.

percentage change, so that the sum of the logarithmic factors equals the total.

As shown in the bottom row of the table, the 2005 optimal carbon tax in the current round is higher than the 1999 estimate by a factor of 2.99, which is a logarithmic difference of 109 percent. The major contributor to this increase, shown in row a, is an increase in world output in nominal terms that is 60 percent higher than the earlier estimate. The higher level of world output arises from two sources that are approximately equal. The first, shown in row $a1$, is that 32 percent of the increase in world output is inflation, that is, simply because of moving from 1990 prices to 2005 prices. The second and more surprising source, shown in row $a2$, comes from moving from market exchange rates (MER) to purchasing-power-parity (PPP) exchange rates as a measure for output, which leads to a 29 percent change in estimated world output. This change reflects the fact that the earlier MER-based estimates effectively underweighted the income level to which the damage function applies. The final (very small) term shown in row $a3$ is the combination of projection errors (actual minus predicted) for individual countries and the composition effects, which subtract 1 percent from world output.

A second contribution to this increase comes from the change in the damage function, which contributes 64 percentage points to the carbon tax, as shown in row b. This increase comes primarily because the new DICE model reduces the estimated economic benefits of warming at low rates of warming for some regions. The difference can be seen in Figure 3-3.

The discount factor over a 20-year period contributes −27 percent to the higher carbon tax, as shown in row c. The negative contribution of the discount rate arises because we have raised our estimate of the real return on goods in the current modeling runs. The final factor is the temperature-sensitivity coefficient, shown in row d, which is raised slightly and contributes 3 percent to the increase in the carbon tax in the simplified model.

The sum of these four factors, shown in row e, totals 100 logarithmic percent. This compares with an increase of 109 percent in the calculated carbon tax in DICE-2007 relative to DICE/RICE-1999. We have not attempted to further decompose the difference between the two DICE-model estimates.

In summary, there has been a major increase in the estimated optimal nominal carbon tax since the last round of estimates. About one-quarter is due to inflation, one-quarter is caused by moving to a PPP output base, and the balance is primarily due to a higher damage function. Other factors sum up to approximately zero in their effects.

VI
The Economics of Participation

Analytical Background

One of the important features of public goods like global warming is that there are widely disparate incentives to participate in measures to mitigate the damages. The differences reflect different perceptions of damages, income levels, political structures, environmental attitudes, and country sizes. For example, Russia may believe that it will benefit from at least limited warming, while India may believe that it will be significantly harmed. The structures of the Framework Convention on Climate Change (which requires only the participation of high-income countries) and the Kyoto Protocol (which excludes major developing countries in principle and the United States in practice) indicate that a realistic analysis of policies must allow for differing national or sectoral rates of participation in international agreements. As a result, without some mechanism to capture differential participation, global models will miss important aspects of nationally differentiated strategies.

The standard approach to modeling differential participation is to disaggregate to the level of the decision makers, in this case primarily the nations, although the level might even be subunits like U.S. states. Earlier versions of the DICE/RICE models examined multiple regions and analyzed the effects of differential participation and policies.

The current version introduces a participation function. This allows model runs in which a subset of countries has emissions reductions in a harmonized fashion while the balance of countries undertakes no emissions reductions. Because of the functional form of the abatement-cost equation in the DICE model, we can derive an exact mathematical representation of the result of incomplete (but harmonized) participation. This new specification allows for estimates of the impact of alternative groupings of structures such as the Kyoto Protocol.

We first describe the algebraic derivation of the participation function. Assume that only a fraction of countries participates in the climate protocols, where this group has a fraction of emissions equal to $\varphi(t)$. Assume for expositional purposes that the emissions-output ratios of participants are equal to those of nonparticipants. Define the control rate of the participants as $\mu^P(t)$, while the control rate of nonparticipants is $\mu^{NP}(t) = 0$. A critical part of the model is that the marginal costs of emissions are equated among participants, say, through emissions trading. Then the abatement cost of participants, $\Psi^P(t)$, and the aggregate cost, $\Psi(t)$, are given by

$$\Psi(t) = \Psi^P(t) = Q^P(t)\theta_1(t)\mu^P(t)^{\theta_2},$$

where $Q^P(t)$, $Q^{NP}(t)$, and $Q(t)$ are the output levels of participating and nonparticipating countries and the global total, while $\theta_1(t)$ and θ_2 are parameters of the abatement-cost function (see the Appendix for definitions of the variables). The overall control rate is given by

$$\mu(t) = \mu^P(t)\varphi(t).$$

Substituting, and recalling that $Q^P(t) = Q(t)\varphi(t)$, we get

$$\Psi(t) = \{Q(t)\varphi(t)\}\theta_1(t)\{\mu(t)/\varphi(t)\}^{\theta_2}$$
$$= Q(t)\theta_1(t)\mu(t)^{\theta_2}\varphi(t)^{1-\theta_2}.$$

This compares with a complete-participation abatement-cost function of

$$\Psi(t) = Q(t)\theta_1(t)\mu(t)^{\theta_2}.$$

Therefore, with incomplete participation, abatement costs for a given global control rate rise by the factor $\pi(t) = \varphi(t)^{1-\theta_2}$ where $\pi(t)$ is the "participation-cost markup." There is an inefficiency induced by nonparticipation; the inefficiency is an exponential function of the parameter $(\theta_2 - 1)$, which represents the convexity of the marginal-cost-of-abatement function. If marginal costs are constant (which makes no economic sense), the parameter $(\theta_2 - 1)$ is zero and there is no penalty from incomplete participation. On the other hand, if the marginal-cost function is rising with higher abatement (as is found in virtually all studies), and $(\theta_2 - 1) > 0$, and particularly if it is convex (as is suggested by most empirical cost studies), then incomplete participation is costly.[1]

Applications

We provide three illustrations of how participation matters to the efficiency of a policy. Begin with the example of the Kyoto

Protocol. The major result of our analysis is that the Kyoto Protocol is an expensive and inefficient approach, given the high costs and meager rewards. We can see why this is the case by using the participation function, which was used in the modeling of the Protocol.

Annex I countries, including the United States, were responsible for about 66 percent of global CO_2 emissions in 1990. We estimate that the exponent of the cost function is $\theta_2 = 2.8$. With 66 percent participation, the cost of incomplete participation was $(0.66)^{-1.8} = 2.1$ times the cost with complete participation (here complete participation is the same as global trading).[2] However, by 2010, the participation rate (with the U.S. withdrawal and the increasing share of developing countries) is estimated to be about 33 percent. The cost with incomplete participation is estimated to be $(0.33)^{-1.8} = 7.4$ times the cost of the same global emissions reduction with full participation.

As another example, we can look at how the optimal policy depends upon the participation rate. For this experiment, we allow the participation rate to vary exogenously from 0 to 100 percent. For reference purposes, the original Kyoto Protocol covered about 66 percent of 1990 emissions, whereas the current Protocol is estimated to cover about 33 percent of emissions for 2010. In an optimal policy, the global average carbon tax and control rate will decline as participation falls. For this experiment, we optimize carbon emissions, the global carbon tax, and the emissions-control rate for the exogenous participation rate.

Figure 6-1 shows the optimal global carbon tax in 2015 as a function of the participation rate. The optimal carbon tax for 100 percent participation is $42 per ton (the value shown in Table 5-4). However, note that the equivalent global carbon tax falls more than proportionally with participation because

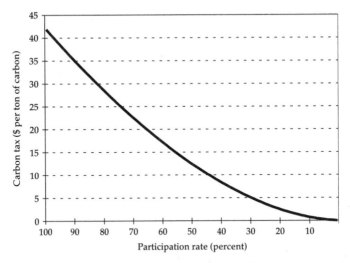

Figure 6-1. Globally averaged carbon tax as a function of partici-pation rate, 2015. These special runs calculate the optimal policies as a function of the global participation rate. This figure shows how the 2015 globally averaged carbon tax varies with the participation rate. The carbon tax of the participants is virtually unchanged as the par-ticipation rate changes.

of the convexity of the cost function. Figure 6-2 shows the loss in welfare that arises from incomplete participation. This re-sult shows again how important full participation is. Even if a perfectly efficient policy is designed and implemented, a substantial fraction of the potential gains will be lost if there is incomplete participation.

A third application is to ask how close we can get to the global optimum with an architecture that limits emissions con-trols to major countries. This proposal is somewhat in the spirit of the Bush administration's May 2007 proposal in which it laid out a plan for an agreement on climate change among 10 to 15

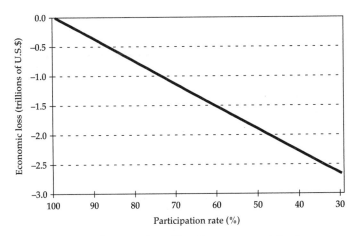

Figure 6-2. Loss of economic welfare from nonparticipation.

large emitters.[3] We calculate the cost penalty that arises from limiting the scope of the policy to a subset of countries. Using the formula developed earlier, we can calculate the ratio of the cost of achieving a policy with limited participation to the cost with universal participation. Table 6-1 shows the results of the calculations. For this purpose, we have used constant 2004 emissions to estimate the cost of nonparticipation. Our estimate is that for these groupings, the shares of the large countries in global emissions are relatively stable over the next few decades as long as the large developing countries are included.

According to our estimates, limiting participation to the big five emitters (the United States, China, Russia, India, and Germany) would cover a little more than half of global emissions. The cost penalty would be a factor of around 3. This indicates that obtaining a given climatic objective, such as temperature or concentration stabilization, would cost three times as much if the agreement were limited to the big five. At the other end, we

Table 6-1. Penalty from Limiting Agreements
to Large Countries

A. Fraction of global emissions	
Big five countries	0.528
Big four countries plus WE	0.632
All major (EU plus big nine)	0.749
B. Cost penalty (ratio to complete participation)	
Big five countries	3.16
Big four countries plus WE	2.29
All major (EU plus big nine)	1.68

Note: Big five are United States, China, Russia, India, and Germany. Big four are United States, China, Russia, and India. WE includes only Western European members of EU. Big nine includes big four plus Brazil, Canada, Japan, Mexico, and South Africa. Part A of the table shows the fraction of 2005 global CO_2 emissions that come from the different groups. Part B shows the cost penalty associated with partial participation. For example, if only the big five countries are included, this would cover 53 percent of emissions, and the cost penalty for attaining a given global emissions reduction would be a factor of 3.16.

include the European Union and the big nine (which include the big four non-European countries plus Brazil, Canada, Japan, Mexico, and South Africa). Including these countries would expand an agreement to cover 75 percent of emissions; this would lead to a cost penalty of 68 percent.

All these experiments reinforce the point that for an additive global public good like reducing global warming by emissions reductions, achieving a high level of participation is important. The final experiment suggests that including the major countries or groupings can move a substantial way toward the goals of complete participation.

VII
Dealing with Uncertainty in Climate-Change Policy

General Background on Uncertainty

Behavioral studies have repeatedly shown that people overestimate their confidence in their knowledge of the world. Not only do people underestimate the range of possible outcomes, but they also often forget that there are forces that they have not thought about, or do not know about, that will upset their plans and expectations. The overconfidence problem can easily arise in analytical studies, such as computerized approaches like the DICE model, where the results are shown with great precision and with many significant digits. How confident can we be in the results of our modeling? What are the implications for climate-change policy of accounting for uncertainties? These topics are addressed in this chapter.

What do we mean by uncertainty? In the present context, we have a complex system that is imperfectly understood in the sense that we are unsure how the system will evolve in the future. The uncertainty is based on incomplete knowledge about external variables and about the system itself. For the first of these, there are outside or exogenous forces (such as population or GHG concentrations) that we can measure, perhaps imperfectly, for the past, but can only project with error for the future. Second, there are the natural and societal systems that take these exogenous influences and generate variables of importance, such as output, emissions, climate change, and impacts. The forms of these equations, as well as their parameters, are not completely known and in some cases, such as impacts, may hardly be known at all.

We can simplify by assuming that all these systems are represented by a (potentially very large) number of parameters. These parameters might be population, temperature sensitivity, the amount of carbon in the biosphere, the rate of technological change for renewable resources, and so forth. The purpose of uncertainty analysis is, first, to identify a manageable set of parameters to investigate; second, to estimate the potential distribution of each of the important parameters; and third, to estimate the impact of the parameter uncertainties on important questions. For the DICE model, we have initially boiled the climatic-economic system down to 17 important equations and 44 important parameters. In this chapter, we further limit the analysis to eight major uncertainties.

We should pause to describe the nature of the probabilities that are used here. These are not "objective" or "frequentist" probabilities, such as might be observed from long time series on stock-market returns or mortality rates. Rather, they are "subjective" or "judgmental" probabilities, stemming from the approach developed by Frank Ramsey (1931) and L. J. Savage (1954). Judgmental probabilities are ones that are held by individuals and are based on formal or informal reasoning about phenomena, rather than solely on observed events.

It is generally necessary to use judgmental probabilities in analyses of climate change because there are limited or no historical observations on which to base assessments of the parameters of concern. We cannot, for example, estimate the economic impact of a 3°C rise in global temperature from historical data because nothing resembling that kind of global change has occurred in the historical record of human societies. There is no single methodology for determining judgmental probabilities; researchers rely on a variety of techniques, including personal judgments, betting markets, surveys of experts, and comparisons of results from alternative models or theories, to provide information for the underlying distributions.

A growing body of literature examines the impacts of climate-change uncertainty. This analysis has three general purposes: first, we might simply want to know how uncertain the future is for the major variables; second, we might want to examine the implications of uncertainty for climate-change policies; finally, we might consider the impact on both our projections and our policies of learning about the economic and natural systems. In the present chapter, we examine only the first two of these three topics. We then conclude with some reflections on the implications of potentially catastrophic outcomes.

Technical Background for the Estimates

In undertaking an analysis of the uncertainty of the system, the first step is to determine which of the many possible uncertainties we wish to examine. On the basis of earlier studies using the DICE model, as well as studies by other scholars, we have selected eight of the major parameters in the DICE model for further study: uncertainties about the growth rate of total factor productivity, the rate of decarbonization, population growth, the cost of the backstop technology, the damage-output coefficient, the atmospheric retention fraction of carbon dioxide, the temperature-sensitivity coefficient, and the total availability of fossil fuels. Earlier studies have shown that these parameters have the largest impact on both outcomes and policies.

For each of these parameters, we have estimated the distribution of the subjective probability of the parameter on the basis of the scientific or economic uncertainty. Table 7-1 summarizes the assumptions about the uncertain parameters. It should be emphasized that these distributions are indeed judgmental and have been estimated by the author. Other researchers would make, and other studies have made, different assessments of the values of these parameters.

We illustrate the estimation of parameter uncertainty for the temperature-sensitivity parameter (TSP). One important set of estimates of the TSP is from the different models that were reviewed by the IPCC Fourth Assessment Report (IPCC 2007b). This report indicates that the 16 different Atmosphere-Ocean General Circulation Models (AOGCMs) have a mean TSP of 3.3°C, with a standard deviation of that mean of 0.7°C (p. 631). We also examine a time-series estimate using the DICE climate-model specification and the historical data on CO_2 and other forcings and global mean temperature. This yielded an estimate of the TSP of 2.1°C with a standard error of the coefficient of 0.53°C. Combining these likelihood functions, we obtain a joint estimate of 2.8°C with a standard error of 0.5°C. This joint estimate is reasonably close to the IPCC central estimate of 3.0°C. For the uncertainty runs, we doubled the combined standard error based on the presumption that the models and empirical estimates are likely to underestimate the uncertainty. This procedure yields the figure shown in Table 7-1. Below we discuss alternative estimates where the distributions are not normal.

Table 7-1. Major Assumptions about Uncertain Parameters in Uncertainty Runs

Variable	Definition	Units	Mean	Standard Deviation
g(TFP)	Rate of growth of total factor productivity	Per year	0.0092	0.0040
g(CO_2/GDP)	Rate of decarbonization	Per year	−0.007	0.002
T2 × CO_2	Equilibrium temperature-sensitivity coefficient	°C per CO_2 doubling	3.00	1.11
DamCoeff	Damage parameter (intercept of damage equation)	Fraction of global output	0.0028	0.0013
P(back)	Price of backstop technology	$ per ton of carbon replaced	1,170	468
Pop	Asymptotic global population	Millions	8,600	1,892
CarCyc	Transfer coefficient in carbon cycle	Per decade	0.189	0.017
Fosslim	Total resources of fossil fuels	Billions of tons of carbon	6,000	1,200

Note: The mean values and standard deviations of the uncertain parameters used in this chapter. For a detailed discussion of the derivation of the parameters, see "Accompanying Notes and Documentation of DICE-2007 Model" (Nordhaus 2007a).

We then make 100 runs of the DICE model using random draws of the eight parameters, where it is assumed that the uncertain variables are distributed independently and with normal probability distributions, and we rule out parameters with the wrong sign. We assume normal distributions primarily because we fully understand their properties. We recognize that there are substantial reasons to prefer other distributions for some variables, particularly ones that are skewed or have "fat tails," but introducing other distributions is highly speculative at this stage and is a more ambitious topic than the limited analyses that are undertaken here, for which the normal distribution will suffice.

We can describe the uncertainty estimates analytically as follows. In these calculations, we project the major variables for the baseline (no-controls) case assuming that the uncertain variables take a given set of values. (The notation in this description is slightly different from that in the rest of this book.) Let y_t be the endogenous variables (output, emissions, and so on.), z_t be the exogenous and nonstochastic variables (other greenhouse gases, land-based emissions, and so on), and $\theta = [\theta_1, \ldots, \theta_8]$ be the eight uncertain parameters (growth rate of total factor productivity, population growth, and so on). Then we can represent the structure of the DICE model schematically as

$$(7.1) \quad y_t = H(z_t; \theta),$$

where $H(z_t; \theta)$ represents the structure of the DICE model.

Earlier chapters assumed that the uncertain parameters took their expected values, $\theta^* = E(\theta)$. In this chapter, we assume that the uncertain parameters are normally distributed, $\theta \approx N(\theta^*, \sigma_t)$, with mean $= \theta^*$ and estimated or subjective standard deviation $= \sigma_t$. For the uncertain runs, we take 100 random draws of the eight uncertain parameters from their distributions, yielding realizations $\theta^{(i)} = [\theta_1^{(i)}, \ldots, \theta_8^{(i)}]$, $i = 1, \ldots, 100$. We then run the DICE model with each of the realizations, yielding 100 random runs:

(7.2) $y_t^{(i)} = H(z_t; \theta^{(i)})$.

We then calculate the distribution of the outcomes of the 100 random runs. Note that there are slight differences between the runs shown here and in earlier chapters because we have simplified the model slightly to facilitate computations.

Importance of Different Uncertainties

We begin by calculating the impact of different uncertain variables on the major outcomes in the DICE model. For these experiments, we take the baseline run and then vary each uncertain parameter. We examine a grid of values that range from -6 normal standard deviations to $+6$ normal standard deviations. Tables 7-2 and 7-3 show the calculations for two important variables: the social cost of carbon for 2005 and global CO_2 emissions for 2100. Each table shows the value of these outcome variables as each of the uncertain variables is changed from its mean value to its mean plus sigma times the number of normal standard deviations shown in the first column. We show only the effects in one direction because the results are sufficiently linear that this displays the patterns accurately.

The last two columns provide a range of associated probabilities that indicate how likely or unlikely a parameter might be given our associated knowledge about the parameter. More precisely, these columns show the probability that the uncertain variable would be at least as far from the central value as that assumed value for a normal distribution and for a t-distribution. For example, the probability that a normal variable would be at least 3 sigmas (standard deviations) from the mean value is 0.0013. Similarly, the probability that the values would exceed 5 sigmas is 3×10^{-7} if the

Table 7-2. Uncertainty Results for the Social Cost of Carbon, 2005

| | Value of SCC for Different Uncertain Parameters | | | | | | | | Prob (x > x*) | |
| | (2005 $ per Ton of Carbon in 2005) | | | | | | | | | |
Sigma	g(TFP)	g(CO$_2$/GDP)	T2 × CO$_2$	DamCoeff	P(back)	Pop	CarCyc	Fosslim	Normal	t(5)
0	28.10	28.10	28.10	28.10	28.10	28.10	28.10	28.10	0.5000	0.5000
1	36.07	28.27	38.07	40.99	28.10	32.14	29.16	28.10	0.1587	0.2047
2	48.08	28.43	46.44	53.89	28.10	35.91	30.32	28.10	0.0228	0.0579
3	51.21	28.60	53.49	66.80	28.10	39.44	31.61	28.10	0.0013	0.0169
4	54.68	28.76	59.47	79.73	28.10	42.75	33.04	28.10	3.17 E-05	0.0057
5	58.52	28.92	64.59	92.66	28.10	45.84	34.62	28.10	2.87 E-07	0.0022
6	62.80	29.09	69.03	105.61	28.11	48.75	36.39	28.10	9.87 E-10	0.0010

Note: The value of the social cost of carbon is shown for the mean values of the parameters and for the mean plus sigma times the number of standard deviations in the "sigma" column. Each column shows the results from varying only the listed parameter while holding all other parameters at their mean value. We have varied the parameter in the direction in which the social cost of carbon increases. For example, if the damage coefficient is one standard deviation above its mean, then the social cost of carbon is $40.99 per ton of carbon rather than $28.10 per ton of carbon at its mean value.

Variable key:

Sigma = number of standard deviations from the mean; g(TFP) = growth in total factor productivity; g(CO$_2$/GDP) = rate of decarbonization; T2 × CO$_2$ = temperature-sensitivity coefficient; DamCoeff = intercept of damage function; P(back) = price of backstop technology; Pop = asymptotic population; CarCyc = atmospheric fraction in carbon cycle; Fosslim = resource abundance of carbon fuels; Prob (x > x*) = probability that value will exceed the value at that level of sigma for normal and Student's t distribution with 5 degrees of freedom.

Table 7-3. Uncertainty Results for Global CO_2 Emissions, 2100

Global CO_2 Emissions for Different Uncertain Parameters, 2100

(Billions of Tons Carbon per Year)

Sigma	g(TFP)	g(CO$_2$/GDP)	T2×CO$_2$	DamCoeff	P(back)	Pop	CarCyc	Fosslim	Prob (x>x*) Normal	t(5)
0	19.08	19.08	19.08	19.08	19.08	19.08	19.08	19.08	0.5000	0.5000
1	30.99	21.95	19.18	19.18	19.08	22.84	19.08	19.08	0.1587	0.2047
2	50.19	25.19	19.28	19.28	19.08	26.42	19.09	19.08	0.0228	0.0579
3	78.20	28.83	19.38	19.38	19.08	29.84	19.10	19.08	0.0013	0.0169
4	103.92	32.91	19.48	19.48	19.08	33.06	19.10	19.08	3.17 E-05	0.0057
5	65.19	37.36	19.59	19.59	19.07	36.08	19.10	19.08	2.87 E-07	0.0022
6	24.61	42.22	19.70	19.70	19.07	38.90	19.11	19.08	9.87 E-10	0.0010

Note: The estimated CO_2 emissions in 2100 for both the mean values of the parameters and for the mean plus sigma times the number of standard deviations in the "sigma" column. Each column shows the results from varying only the listed parameter while holding all other parameters at their mean value. For example, if the rate of total factor productivity is two standard deviations above its mean, then the estimated emissions are 50.2 billion tons of carbon per year rather than 19.1 billion in the baseline projection. Note that emissions turn down for high sigmas of the productivity growth rate because fossil fuels are nearly exhausted by 2100.

Variable key:

Sigma = number of standard deviations from the mean; g(TFP) = growth in total factor productivity; g(CO_2/GDP) = rate of decarbonization; T2 × CO_2 = temperature-sensitivity coefficient; DamCoeff = intercept of damage function; P(back) = price of backstop technology; Pop = asymptotic population; CarCyc = atmospheric fraction in carbon cycle; Fosslim = resource abundance of carbon fuels; Prob (x > x*) = probability that value will exceed the value at that level of sigma for normal and Student's t distribution with 5 degrees of freedom; nc = not calculated.

variable is distributed as a normal variable. Additionally, we show the p-values for a t-distribution with 5 degrees of freedom, shown as $t(5)$. This distribution would be appropriate if we estimated the parameter from a small sample of observations and had no other useful information about the parameter. For the $t(5)$ distribution, which is a "medium-fat-tailed distribution," the 5-sigma probability is 0.0022.

We also show in Figure 7-1 the effect of uncertainty about different parameters on the global temperature increase between 1900 and 2100. This figure indicates that the cost of the backstop technology, the damage coefficient, and the fossil-fuel resource limits are unimportant for the uncertainty about global temperature increase. The unimportance is indicated by the flat line for those variables, which indicates that even out to six sigmas, there is no discernible effect on the temperature increase through 2100.

By far the most important uncertain variable for climatic outcomes is the growth in total factor productivity. The reason is that total factor productivity is the main driver of economic growth in the long run, and output trends tend to dominate emissions trends and therefore climate change. For this reason, productivity is the most important uncertain variable. The second most important variable, which is not surprising, is the temperature-sensitivity coefficient. Moderately important variables are population growth, the rate of decarbonization, and the carbon cycle.

Two major points should be drawn from these parametric calculations. First, there are indeed major uncertainties about future projections. The most important uncertainty surrounds the growth of productivity, and variables such as the temperature-sensitivity coefficient, population growth, and the rate of decarbonization are of second-level importance.

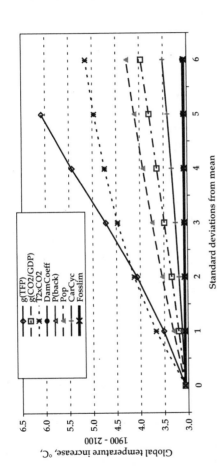

Figure 7-1. Global temperature increase as a function of uncertain parameters. The estimated global mean temperature increase from 1900 to 2100 for the mean value of each parameter and for the values at the given number of standard deviations are shown on the horizontal axis.

Variable key (for detailed definitions, see Table 7-1): g(TFP) = growth in total factor productivity; g(CO_2/GDP) = rate of decarbonization; T2 × CO_2 = temperature-sensitivity coefficient; DamCoeff = intercept of damage function; P(back) = price of backstop technology; Pop = asymptotic population; CarCyc = atmospheric fraction in carbon cycle; Fosslim = resource abundance of carbon fuels.

Second, the uncertainties appear to be linear in their level of uncertainty. In other words, the impact of a $2k$-sigma change in the parameter is generally close to two times the impact of a k-sigma change in the parameter. The exception comes at thresholds, such as when the price of the backstop is close to zero, or when fossil fuels are exhausted.

Applications

We next turn to an examination of the impact of all the uncertain variables taken together. These may produce unexpected results because of interactions among the variables and the nonlinearity of the DICE model.

The first step is to estimate the uncertainty of the projections in the DICE model taking all the uncertainties together. Figures 7-2 and 7-3 show two results from this experiment. Figure 7-2 shows the uncertainty bands for the global mean temperature increase from the present through 2155. The figure shows the most likely result (which is the certainty equivalent analyzed in earlier chapters) and the mean of the 100 runs, as well as the mean plus and minus one standard deviation (the two-sigma range). For normal variables, the two-sigma range shown in the figures will cover about 68 percent of the possible outcomes. These simulations indicate that the 68 percent confidence range for the temperature increase from 1900 to 2155 is between 2.5°C and 6.0°C. This uncertainty is clearly very large.

Figure 7-3 shows estimates of the social cost of carbon (SCC) generated by the random draws in the baseline run. Looking at the current (2005) social cost of carbon, we see that the mean estimate ($26.85 per ton) is slightly less than the most likely estimate ($28.10 per ton). This important finding

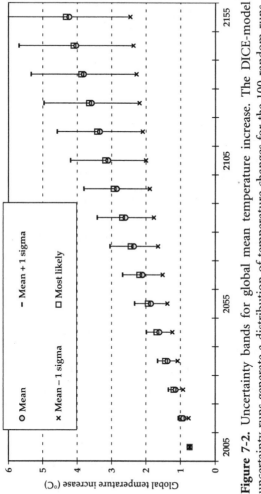

Figure 7-2. Uncertainty bands for global mean temperature increase. The DICE-model uncertainty runs generate a distribution of temperature changes for the 100 random runs. This figure shows the mean of the 100 runs, the certainty equivalent ("most likely"), and the means plus and minus one standard deviation of the runs.

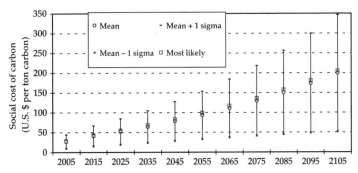

Figure 7-3. Uncertainty bands for the social cost of carbon. The current uncertainty bands for the social cost of carbon at different dates in the future. The square and circle in the center of the bars are, respectively, the certainty equivalent for the SSC and the mean SSC for the 100 runs. See Figure 7-2 for a description of the display.

indicates that the estimates in the certainty-equivalent model are very close to the estimates in the uncertainty model.[1] The second finding is that the two-sigma range (the mean plus and minus one standard deviation) for the SCC in 2005 is $9.62 to $44.09 per ton of carbon. We also showed in Chapter 3 (see Figure 3-2) the uncertainty range for baseline global CO_2 emissions that is generated by this same procedure.

To test for the empirical significance of the assumption of normal distributions, we do a further set of runs using an alternative distribution for the temperature sensitivity coefficient (TSC). For these runs, we used the likelihood function generated by the time-series estimate of the TSC described above. For these estimates, the likelihood function is indeed asymmetric (right-skewed). We took an alternative distribution for the TSC by adjusting the likelihood function to be equal to the mean and standard deviation of the TSC in the original uncertainty runs but with the asymmetry in the estimated distribution. We then re-estimated all the outcome variables for an additional 100 runs. In this alternative, there were very small changes in the distribution of most variables. However, because of the skewness of the TSC and the nonlinearity of the damage function, the average level of damages was higher. Consequently, the social cost of carbon in the baseline was also higher by about 1 percent. While these results are hardly definitive, they suggest that adjusting coefficients to conform to a non-normal distribution may have only a small effect on the results as long as the means and standard deviations are correctly estimated.

What is the appropriate interpretation of these results? They should not be interpreted as saying that nature herself is subject to such large random forces. Rather, the appropriate interpretation is that our knowledge about nature's forces in the distant future is extremely limited. These results say that we would have reasonable confidence (roughly a two-in-three chance) that the actual paths of the variables lie within the ranges shown in the figures, but with current information (at least as estimated by the author) we cannot improve the precision of these projections. Better science, economics, and monitoring and the passage of time will narrow these uncertainties in the years to come.

Should High-Climate-Change Outcomes Have a Risk Premium?

A further application of the uncertainty runs investigates the important question of the risk properties of high-climate-change outcomes. The issue here is whether economies should be risk averse to outcomes where climate change is at the high end. At first blush, the answer is obviously yes. High-climate-change scenarios—where the temperature change is 3 or 4 or 5°C and the potential for major-damage thresholds appears—would seem to be ones for which we would pay high insurance premiums. After all, these outcomes are the climatic equivalent of many of our houses burning down, which we would pay a lofty risk premium to avoid.

On further reflection, the answer is less obvious. The modern theory of risk and insurance holds that the risk premiums on different outcomes are determined by the correlation of a risk with consumption in different states of the world. This approach, known as the consumption-capital-asset pricing model (CCAPM), looks at the fundamental determinants of risk premiums in a world in which all contingencies are insurable and where there are insurance markets for all types of risk.[2] A situation has adverse risk characteristics and requires a risk premium if the bad outcome occurs when we are relatively poor. So if we are likely to be relatively poor when our house burns down (which seems to be an obvious situation, compared with when our house is intact), we should pay a risk premium for fire insurance. However, if an event were to occur only when we were very rich, such as the risk of someone stealing a billion-dollar painting from our house in 20 years, then we would not be well advised to pay a risk premium today on art insurance for that event.

Therefore, to determine whether there is a significant risk premium on high-climate-change situations, we need to know whether high-climate-change outcomes are situations in which we are relatively rich or relatively poor. We need a general-equilibrium model that generates the uncertain outcomes and provides the accompanying consumption level, which is just what the DICE-model runs do. Suppose that high climate change occurs only when we are rich and can therefore particularly well afford to bear the risks. In this case, we would generally not want to redistribute income from a low-income outcome to a high-income outcome by paying a large insurance premium to reduce risks in the high-income, high-climate-change outcome.

The answer to whether we should pay a risk premium on bad climate outcomes therefore depends upon the correlation of our income (or technically, the marginal utility of consumption) with the climatic outcome. We can investigate this relationship by examining the correlation between these variables for the 100 random runs. Figure 7-4 shows the plot of

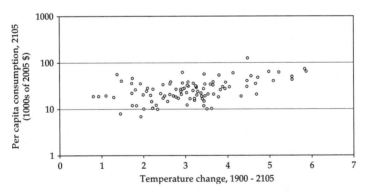

Figure 7-4. Temperature change and consumption, 2105. The vertical axis shows projected per capita consumption in 2105 for the 100 random runs. The horizontal axis shows the temperature change associated with each run. The results suggest that high-climate-change scenarios are ones with high levels of consumption per capita.

per capita consumption and temperature increase for the 100 runs in the year 2105, but similar plots hold for other years as well. The surprising result here is that high-climate-change outcomes are positively correlated with consumption. This implies that high-climate-change outcomes are negatively correlated with the marginal utility of consumption (because of the declining marginal utility of consumption with increasing consumption). Those states in which the global temperature increase is particularly high are also ones in which we are on average richer in the future. This leads to the paradoxical result that there is actually a negative risk premium on high-climate-change outcomes.

The reason for this surprising result is that the major factor that produces different climate outcomes in our uncertainty runs is differential technological change. According to the uncertainty-analysis parameters shown in Table 7-1, the uncertainty about total factor productivity growth is estimated to be 0.4 percent per year, which leads to a two-standard-deviation uncertainty factor of 2.2 over a century and 4.9 over two centuries. In our estimates, the productivity uncertainty outweighs the uncertainties of the climate system and the damage function in determining the relationship between temperature change and consumption.

This result clearly depends upon the estimates of uncertainty for different parameters and should be estimated using different models. But the major point is that we cannot simply say in parrot-like fashion, "Bad climate, high risk premium." The size and sign of the risk premium will depend upon the sources of the risk. The negative risk premium found here reminds us that the riskiness of different scenarios should be viewed in the context of a complete model of the determination of the risk premium, and that simply looking at bad scenarios in a partial-equilibrium framework misses the question of what determines the uncertainties and bad scenarios in the first place.

We can put this point differently by grouping the random runs into the 50 runs with the highest temperature increase in 2100 ("high climate change") and the 50 runs with the lowest temperature increase ("low climate change"). The high-climate-change cases have an average temperature increase of 3.9°C by 2100, while the low-climate-change cases have an average temperature increase of 2.5°C. Climate damages are 4.4 percent of output in the high case and 1.6 percent of output in the low case, with an average damage output of 3.0 percent.

We might suppose that the 3.0 percent should be increased because of risk aversion against the prospects of the high-climate-change case. However, this reasoning is incorrect. The world is projected to be richer in the high-climate-change state than in the low-climate-change state: in the random runs, per capita consumption is 40 percent higher in the high-climate-change state. With our assumed utility function, the marginal utility of consumption in the high state is about half that in the low state (this is different than would be calculated from the averages of the subsamples because of nonlinearities). If we weight the damage ratios by the marginal utility of consumption for all states, then the marginal-utility-weighted average damage ratio is not equal to the average ratio of 3.0 percent of output, or perhaps to some higher number, but is instead equal to 2.1 percent of output. In other words, the risk-weighted damage ratio is below the certainty-equivalent damage ratio.

It should be emphasized that this back-of-the-envelope calculation is not the recommended approach for doing risk analysis. The appropriate way is to go back to basics and maximize the expected value of utility, taking into account the entire range of uncertainties. For example, if we want to know the expected social cost of carbon, we should not apply some risk premium to the distribution. Rather, we should look at the calculations behind Figure 7-3, which shows that the expected value of the SCC is actually below the certainty equivalent. The reason for this result is similar to the reason why there is the apparent negative risk premium. The major point is that doing shortcut calculations such as applying a risk premium to outcomes can produce incorrect results unless there is a full assessment of the reasons for the uncertainty.

A homey example might clarify this paradox. Assume that in the future low-economic-growth outcome, we are living in caves, while in the future high-economic-growth outcome we have four stately mansions. As a result of global warming associated with the high-growth outcome, one of our four mansions burns down, while on the low-growth path, our caves remain unscathed. What kind of risk premium should we pay today to cover the high damages to our mansions in the high-growth, high-loss case? Given that the costs today will have a larger utility impact on our well-being in the low-growth cave state and will not affect our shelter in the cave outcome, we should be advised to underweight the loss of one of our four stately mansions.

This fanciful example may seem irrelevant for the serious issues of risk and climate change. While we are probably not thinking about mansions versus caves in 2100, the underlying analytical point is important. If damages arise predominantly because of rapid economic growth, then we might well have a negative risk premium on high-damage states.

Abrupt and Catastrophic Climate Change

Before concluding this discussion of uncertainty, we consider the issues raised by abrupt and catastrophic climate change. Over the past decade, scientists have discovered that the climate system is much more variable than had earlier been supposed. This new view has been examined in the literature on abrupt climate change. Among the remarkable discoveries is that the global climate system appears to have switched between climatic states, which may differ by as much as half an ice age in magnitude, in a period of one or two decades.[3]

The discoveries about abrupt climate change have led to concerns that there may be grave or even catastrophic implications of the magnitude of climate changes that are being triggered by the current trajectory of emissions. An early concern was that warming would in the near future lead to an abrupt shutdown of Atlantic deepwater circulation. However, the most recent IPCC assessment concluded that "it is very unlikely that the [Atlantic deepwater circulation] will undergo a large abrupt transition during the course of the 21st century."[4] However, the Fourth Assessment also suggests that the melting of the Greenland ice sheet over 1,000 years might provide a flow of freshwater that is equivalent to the quantity estimated to trigger shutdowns of Atlantic deepwater circulation in the past or in model estimates.[5]

Perhaps the most prominent concern today is that warming will trigger forces that will lead to further accelerated warming and then to rapid melting of the Greenland ice sheet and parts of the Antarctic ice sheets. The geological record indicates that ice-sheet collapse in the past has caused sea-level increases of up to 20 meters in less than 500 years.[6] The most recent IPCC report provides the following summary of the outlook for the Greenland ice sheet (which contains approximately 7 meters of sea-level equivalent): "A threshold of annual mean warming of 1.9°C to 4.6°C in Greenland has been estimated for elimination of the [Greenland ice sheet] . . . , a process which would take many centuries to complete."[7] The West Antarctic ice sheet, which contains approximately 6 meters of sea-level equivalent, is vulnerable, but, according to the IPCC report, "Present understanding is insufficient for prediction of the possible speed or extent of such a collapse."[8]

Although it is difficult to envision the ecological and societal consequences of the melting of these ice sheets, this situation is clearly highly undesirable and should be avoided unless prevention is ruinously expensive. Figure 7-5 provides an estimate of the fraction of the world's population and output that lay below 10 meters of elevation in 1990. Approximately 3 percent of output and 4 percent of population were in this zone.

It has proved extremely difficult until now to estimate the economic impacts of catastrophic climate change. Perhaps the most serious problem is the lack of an accepted scientific understanding of the major potential catastrophic events. The events that have been most carefully studied are the two mentioned earlier, the reversal of Atlantic deepwater circulation and melting of the Greenland and Antarctic ice sheets. However, the Fourth Assessment Report appears to rule these out as likely events over the next century.

This book has included in the damage estimates the potential for catastrophic consequences from abrupt climate change. These are included as a "willingness to pay" to avoid the damages that might accompany major climate changes. For example, at a 6°C climate change, approximately half the estimated damages are to avoid the abrupt and catastrophic damages that might occur. These estimates were derived in

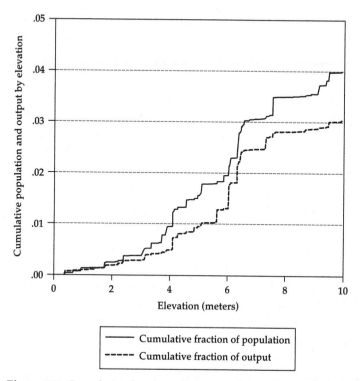

Figure 7-5. Cumulative fraction of output and population by elevation, 1990. The fraction of the world's population and output lying below a given elevation. The resolution is 1° latitude by 1° longitude. (*Source*: GEcon database, available at gecon.yale.edu.)

the studies underlying the DICE/RICE-1999 model. There have been some minor technical modifications of the earlier approach, but the estimated impacts from that study are retained for the DICE-2007 model.

Some analysts have argued that the present approach does not go far enough and that we should include the potential for climate changes to cause major and unacceptable damage to the world economy—the equivalent of a permanent

Great Depression, civilizational collapse, or even human extinction. In a series of recent studies, Richard Tol and Martin Weitzman have suggested that the combination of limited data and inherent uncertainty about the parameters of the climatic-economic system may limit the applicability for global warming of analytical approaches such as the DICE model and other integrated assessment models.

An empirical study by Tol uses the Climate Framework for Uncertainty, Negotiation and Distribution (FUND) model, which is an integrated assessment model that emphasizes impacts, to argue that the uncertainties about climate change are so large that the standard cost-benefit analysis does not apply. The FUND model does not find catastrophic outcomes in the sense of near-zero consumption. Rather, Tol finds that negative economic growth and the consequent negative discount rate lead to an (estimated) infinite variance of the social cost of carbon (marginal net present damage in his terminology).[9]

Weitzman argues that economic analyses such as the present one are overwhelmed by the potentially catastrophic events.[10] His argument relies heavily on the limiting properties of the constant relative risk aversion (CRRA) utility function as consumption approaches zero, along with analytical arguments from statistical first principles emphasizing the potential for "fat tails" for the distributions of uncertain parameters. The essence of his argument is that the potential for economic collapse and even extinction should dominate the policy analysis.[11]

Preliminary runs of the DICE model suggest that it does not display the extreme results shown by Weitzman's theory or Tol's empirical analysis. The analysis of extreme values shown in Tables 7-2 and 7-3 does not reveal any sharp nonlinearities in the uncertain variables. That is, the values of the major variables (such as the social cost of carbon) are close to linear in the value of the uncertain variables. The exception is total factor productivity, which is convex in the value of the parameter because of the nonlinear impact of growth rates on output levels.

We emphasize, however, that models such as the present one have limited utility in looking at the potential for catastrophic events. The reason is that the geophysical modules in the DICE-2007 model are smooth functions that capture the average behavior of ensembles of large geophysical models. Until geophysical modelers develop mechanisms for generating abrupt or catastrophic changes, there is little that economic models such as the present one can do to introduce results based on established scientific findings in integrated assessment models.

In any case, this book has more modest goals. The classical approach of decision theory deployed in this chapter is a useful and well-structured way to analyze policies and future trajectories under conditions of uncertainty. We cannot rule out the potential for catastrophic impacts that might justify trillions of dollars of abatement costs. But fears about low-probability outcomes in the distant future should not impede constructive steps to deal with the high-probability dangers that are upon us today. We should start with the clear and present dangers, after which we can turn to the unclear and distant threats.

VIII
The Many Advantages of Carbon Taxes

Prices versus Quantities for Global Public Goods

In dealing with global public goods like global warming, it is necessary to reach through governments to the multitude of firms and consumers who make the vast number of decisions that affect the ultimate outcome. There are only two mechanisms that can realistically be employed: quantitative limits through government fiat and regulation, and price-based approaches through fees, subsidies, or taxes.[1] This chapter addresses the major differences between the two and explains why price-based approaches have major advantages over quantitative limits.

In the global-warming context, quantitative limits set global targets on the time path of the greenhouse-gas emissions of different countries. Countries can then administer these limits in their own fashion, and the mechanism may allow for the transfer and trading of emissions allowances among countries, as is the case under the Kyoto Protocol and the European Union Emission Trading Scheme. This approach has limited experience under existing international protocols, such as the CFC mechanisms, and broader experience under national trading regimes, such as the U.S. SO_2 allowance-trading program.

The second approach is to use harmonized prices, fees, or taxes as a method of coordinating policies among countries. This approach has no international experience in the environmental arena, although it has considerable national experience in environmental markets in such areas as the U.S. tax on ozone-depleting chemicals. On the other hand, the use of harmonized price-type measures has extensive international experience in fiscal and trade policies, such as the harmonization of taxes in the European Union (EU) and harmonized tariffs in international trade.

Attempts to address climate change through prices rather than quantities have been discussed in a handful of papers in the economics literature,[2] but much careful analysis remains to be done. I will highlight a few of the details.

For concreteness, I will discuss a mechanism called "harmonized carbon taxes." This mechanism is a substitute for binding international or national emissions limits. Under this approach, countries would agree to penalize carbon emissions at an internationally harmonized "carbon price" or "carbon tax." Conceptually, the carbon tax is a dynamically efficient Pigovian tax that balances the marginal social costs and marginal social benefits of additional emissions.

The carbon price might be determined by estimates of the price necessary to limit GHG concentrations or temperature changes below some level thought to be "dangerous interference," or it might be the price that would induce the efficient level of control. For example, if an international agreement were reached that the global temperature increase should be limited to 2°C, then, according to the results of earlier chapters, the harmonized tax would be set at $72 per ton of carbon ($20 per ton of CO_2) for 2015 and would rise at about 3 percent per year during the next decade, assuming full participation. This number could be estimated in several integrated assessment models and should be updated as new information arrives. Because carbon prices would be equalized, the approach would be spatially efficient among those countries that have a harmonized set of taxes. If the carbon-tax trajectory follows the rules for when-efficiency, it would also satisfy intertemporal efficiency.

Many important details would need to be negotiated on burden sharing. It might be reasonable to allow full participation to depend upon each country's level of economic development. For example, countries might be expected to participate fully only when their incomes reach a given threshold (perhaps $10,000 per capita), and poor countries might receive transfers to encourage early and complete participation. If carbon prices are equalized across participating countries, there will be no need for tariffs or border tax adjustments among participants. The issues of sanctions, the location of taxation, international-trade treatment, and transfers to developing countries under a harmonized carbon tax are important details that require discussion and refinement.

The literature on regulatory mechanisms entertains a much richer set of approaches than the polar quantity and price types that are examined here. An important variant is a hybrid system that puts a ceiling on the price of emissions-trading permits by combining a tradable-permit system with a government promise to sell additional permits at a specified price.[3] Price caps were considered and rejected by the Clinton administration in its preparation for the negotiations on the Kyoto Protocol. Hybrid approaches such as these should include floors as well as caps; however, most proposals do not include floors. We return to the hybrids as a possibly useful middle ground in the final section of this chapter.

Comparison of Price and Quantity Approaches

This section compares the performance of quantity and price systems for regulating stock global public goods like global warming. The basic message is that because of its conceptual simplicity, a harmonized carbon tax might prove simpler to design and maintain than a quantity mechanism like the Kyoto Protocol.

SETTING BASELINES FOR PRICES AND QUANTITIES

Quantity limits are particularly troublesome where targets must adapt to differential economic growth, uncertain technological change, and evolving science. These problems have been illustrated well by the Kyoto Protocol, which set its targets 13 years before the date on which the controls became effective (2008–2012) and used baseline emissions from 20 years before the control period. Base-year emissions have become increasingly obsolete as the economic and energy structures—and even the political boundaries—of countries have changed.

The baselines for future budget periods and for new participants will present deep problems for extensions of a quantity regime like the Kyoto Protocol. A natural baseline for the post-2012 period would be a no-controls level of emissions. That level is in practice impossible to calculate or predict with accuracy for countries with abatement policies already in place. Problems would arise over how to adjust baselines for changing conditions and how to take into account the extent of past emissions reductions.

Under a price approach, the natural baseline is a carbon tax or penalty of zero. Countries' efforts are then judged relative to that baseline. It is not necessary to choose a historical base year of emissions. Moreover, there is no asymmetry between early joiners and late joiners, and early participants are not disadvantaged by having their baseline adjusted downward. The question of existing energy taxes does raise complications, however, and I address these later.

TREATMENT OF UNCERTAINTY

Uncertainty pervades climate-change science, economics, and policy. One key difference between price and quantity instruments is how well each adapts to deep uncertainty. A major result from environmental economics is that the relative efficiency of price and quantity regulation depends upon the nature—and more precisely the degree of nonlinearity—of costs and benefits (see Weitzman 1974). If the costs are highly nonlinear compared with the benefits, then price-type regulation is more efficient; conversely, if the benefits are highly nonlinear compared with the costs, then quantity-type regulation is more efficient.

Although this issue has received scant attention in the design of climate-change policies, the structure of the costs and damages in global warming indicates a strong preference for price-type approaches. The reason is that the benefits of emissions reductions are related to the stock of greenhouse gases, while the costs of emissions reductions are related to the flow of emissions. This implies that the marginal costs of emissions reductions are highly sensitive to the level of reductions, while the marginal benefits of emissions reductions are insensitive to the current level of emissions reductions.[4] In the DICE model, the benefit function for emissions of a single decade is essentially linear, while the cost function is highly convex, with an elasticity of close to 3. This combination means that emissions fees or taxes are likely to be much more efficient than quantitative standards or tradable quotas when there is considerable uncertainty.

VOLATILITY OF THE MARKET PRICES OF TRADABLE ALLOWANCES

Uncertainties affect prices. Because supply, demand, and regulatory conditions evolve unpredictably over time, quantity-type regulations are likely to cause volatile trading prices of carbon emissions. Price volatility for allowances is likely to be particularly high because of the complete inelasticity of the supply of permits, along with the highly inelastic demand for permits in the short run.

The history of European trading prices for CO_2 illustrates the extreme volatility of quantity systems. During 2006, trading prices ranged from \$44.47 to \$143.06 per ton of carbon (Point Carbon 2006). The price of allowances fell by more than 70 percent in one month because of new regulatory information.

More extensive evidence on the trading prices of quantitative environmental allowances comes from the history of the U.S. sulfur dioxide (SO_2) emissions-trading program. This program includes an annual auction conducted by the Environmental Protection Agency (EPA), as well as private markets in which firms and individuals can buy and sell allowances. The comparison between SO_2 prices and carbon trading prices is useful because the economic characteristics of the two markets are similar. In both markets, the supply is fixed or nearly fixed in the short run. Moreover, in both markets, the demand for permits (whether for SO_2 or CO_2 emissions) is extremely price-inelastic because it is expensive to substitute other inputs for the fuel containing the sulfur or carbon. To some extent, volatility can be moderated if an agreement allows for banking and borrowing, meaning that firms can save emissions allowances for the future or draw from future allowances. But programs are unlikely to allow borrowing, and banking provides only limited relief from price volatility.

We can gain some insight into the likely functioning of CO_2 allowances by examining the historical volatility of the price of SO_2 allowances. Spot SO_2 prices at the annual EPA auction have varied from a low of $66 per ton in 1996 to a high of $860 per ton in 2005. Futures prices have varied by a factor of 4.7 (see EPA 2006). If we look at the private market, we find that allowance prices varied by a factor of 69 in the 1995–2006 period and by a factor of 12 in the 2001–2006 period. Some changes have been induced by changes in regulatory policies, but that feature would be relevant for the carbon market as well.

We can obtain a more precise measure of variability by calculating the statistical volatility of the prices of SO_2 emissions allowances and comparing them with other volatile prices. Volatility measures the average absolute month-to-month change and is a common approach to indicating the variability and unpredictability of asset prices. Figure 8-1

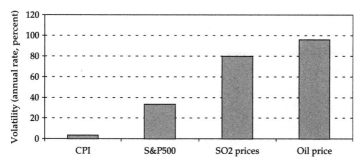

Figure 8-1. Estimated volatility of four prices over the 1995–2006 period. Prices are, from left to right, the consumer price index (CPI), the stock-price index for the Standard and Poor's 500 (S&P500), the price of U.S. SO_2 allowances (SO_2 prices), and the price of crude oil (Oil price). Volatility is calculated as the annualized absolute logarithmic month-to-month change. (*Source*: Oil prices, CPI, and stock prices from DRI database, available from Yale University. Price of SO_2 permits are spot prices provided by Denny Ellerman and reflect the trading prices.)

shows the estimated volatility of four prices for the 1995–2006 period: the consumer price index (CPI), stock prices, SO_2 allowance prices, and oil prices. SO_2 prices are more volatile than stock prices (or the prices of other assets such as houses, which are not shown), they are even more volatile than most consumer prices, and their volatility is close to that of oil prices.

Such rapid fluctuations are costly and undesirable, particularly for an input such as carbon whose aggregate costs might be as great as those of petroleum in the coming decades. An interesting analogue occurred in the United States during the monetarist experiment of 1979–1982, when the Federal Reserve targeted quantities (monetary aggregates) rather than prices (interest rates). During that period, interest rates were extremely volatile. In part because of this increased volatility, the Fed changed back to a price-type approach after a short period of experimentation. This experience suggests that a regime of strict quantity limits might have major disruptive effects on energy markets and on investment planning, as well as on the distribution of income across countries, inflation rates, energy prices, and import and export values. Quantitative limits might consequently become extremely unpopular with market participants and economic policymakers.

PUBLIC-FINANCE QUESTIONS

Another consideration is the fiscal-policy advantage of using revenue-raising measures in restricting emissions. Emissions limits give rise to valuable rights to emit, and the question is whether the government or private parties get the revenues. When taxes or regulatory restrictions raise goods prices, this increases efficiency losses from the existing tax system because the existing tax and regulatory system raises prices above efficient levels. Adding further taxes or regulations on top of existing ones increases the inefficiency or "deadweight loss" of the system, and this increased inefficiency should be counted as part of the additional costs of a global-warming policy. This effect is the "double burden" of taxation, analyzed in the theory of the "double dividend" from green taxes.[5]

If the carbon constraints are imposed through taxes, and the revenues are recycled by reducing taxes on other goods or inputs, then the increased efficiency loss from taxation can be mitigated so that there is no necessary increase in deadweight loss. If the constraints under a quantity-based system are imposed by restrictions that do not raise revenues, however, then there are no government revenues to recycle for reducing the increased deadweight loss. This is an important issue because the efficiency losses can be as large as the abatement costs.

Although it is possible that emissions permits will be auctioned off (thereby generating revenues with which the tax inefficiency can be mitigated), historical practice indicates that most or all permits would be allocated at zero cost to the "deserving" parties, or distributed in such a way as to reduce political resistance. In the cases of SO_2 emission allowances and CFC production allowances, virtually all the permits were allocated at no cost to producers, which yielded no revenues for governments to recycle. Although pure tax systems are the most reliable device for raising revenues, a useful alternative is a hybrid system that would buttress quantity approaches with taxes to capture at least part of the permit revenues.

ISSUES OF EQUITY

Strong and internationally harmonized steps to raise the price of carbon, whether by taxes or by quantitative restrictions, will have substantial impacts on the distribution of income (see Figure 5-11 for an estimate of the resource transfers from consumers). This raises issues of fairness and ability to pay, both among nations and across households within a nation.

Internationally, poor countries would naturally be reluctant to incur the dislocations associated with limiting GHG emissions. To some extent, these can be offset by favorable allocations of emissions permits under a quantitative system. For example, Russia was induced to ratify the original Kyoto Protocol because it had an excess allocation that it believed it could profitably sell in the international market. This would appear to be a major advantage of quantitative systems in promoting fairness among countries.

This advantage may be more apparent than real, more inequitable than equitable, as was seen in the original Kyoto Protocol. Since quotas were set so far in advance, the distribution of burdens across countries is as much lottery as planned and equitable redistribution. Countries such as the United States would be called upon to make higher-than-average reductions because of rapid growth, while countries such as Germany would receive windfall gains because of the historical accident of German reunification. These initial disparities are likely to become embedded in the system because further future reductions start from the original, poorly designed allocations. It is unclear whether in the long run the allocation-plus-lottery aspect of the quantitative system would outweigh the ability to explicitly allocate transfers in a tax-type system.

On the domestic front, a tax system is clearly advantageous relative to an allocation system. The tax system raises substantial revenues. These can be used to alleviate the economic hardships of low-income households through reducing other taxes or increasing benefits. Alternatively, some of the funds could be used for research and development on low-carbon energy systems. By contrast, an allocation system, such as the current cap-and-trade system for SO_2 permits, raises no revenues. There is no natural way to raise funds to alleviate economic burdens or fund energy research. Therefore, with regard to the potential for promoting a fair distribution of burdens and alleviating economic impacts, the tax approach has clear advantages for intranational adjustments, while the international adjustments might be easier in principle, but less clearly so in practice, for the quantitative approach.

RENTS, CORRUPTION, AND THE RESOURCE CURSE

An additional question concerns the administration of programs in a world where governments vary in honesty, transparency, and effective administration. These issues arise with particular force in international environmental agreements, where countries have little domestic incentive to comply, and weak governments may extend corrupt practices to international trading. Quantity-type systems are much more susceptible to corruption than price-type regimes. An emissions-trading system creates valuable international assets in the form of tradable emissions permits and allocates these to countries. Limiting emissions creates a scarcity where none previously existed; it is a rent-creating program. The dangers of quantity approaches compared with price approaches have been demonstrated frequently when quotas have been compared with tariffs in international trade interventions.

Rents lead to rent-seeking behavior. Additionally, resource rents may increase unproductive activity, as well as civil and international wars, and slow economic growth—this being the theory of the "resource curse."[6] The scarce permits could be used by the country's leaders for nonenvironmental purposes such as mansions and monuments rather than to reduce emissions. Dictators and corrupt administrators could sell their permits and pocket the proceeds.

Calculations suggest that tens of billions of dollars' worth of permits may be available for foreign sale from Russia under a tightened Kyoto Protocol. Given our history of privatizing valuable public assets at artificially low prices, it would not be surprising if the carbon market became tangled in corrupt practices, undermining the legitimacy of the process. We might also imagine a revised Kyoto Protocol extended to developing countries. Consider the case of Nigeria, which has had carbon emissions of around 25 million tons in recent years. If Nigeria were allocated tradable allowances equal to recent emissions and could sell them for $40 per ton of carbon, this could raise around $1 billion of hard currency annually in a country whose nonoil exports were only $600 million in 2000.

Problems of financial finagling are not limited to poor, weak, or autocratic states; in the wake of recent accounting scandals, concerns also arise in the United States. A cap-and-trade system relies upon accurate measurements of emissions or fossil-fuel use by sources in participating countries. If firm A (or country A) sells emissions permits to firm B (or country B), where both A and B are operating under caps, then it is essential to monitor the emissions of A and B to make sure that their emissions are within their specified limits. Indeed, if monitoring is ineffective in country A but effective in country B, a trading program could actually end up raising the level of global emissions because A's emissions would remain unchanged while B's emissions would rise. Incentives to evade emissions limitations in an international system are even stronger than the incentives for domestic tax evasion. Tax cheating is a zero-sum game for the company and the government, while emissions-control evasion is a positive-sum game for the two parties involved in the transaction for a global public good.

A price approach gives less room for corruption because it does not create artificial scarcities, monopolies, or rents. There are no permits transferred to countries or leaders of countries, so they cannot be sold abroad for wine or guns. There is no new rent-seeking opportunity. Any revenues would need to be raised by the taxation of domestic fossil-fuel consumption, and a carbon tax would add absolutely nothing to the rent-producing instruments that countries have today. It is a zero-sum game between the government and the taxpayer, so the incentives to ensure enforcement are stronger.

Here again, a hybrid system that combines both tax and quantitative systems would dilute the incentives for corruption in the quantitative system. If the carbon tax is a substantial fraction of the carbon price, then the net value of the permits, and the rents to seek, are accordingly reduced.

ADMINISTRATIVE AND MEASUREMENT ISSUES

Many administrative and measurement issues arise in implementing a harmonized carbon tax, and these have not yet been fully addressed. Perhaps the most important conceptual issue is the treatment of existing energy taxes and subsidies. Should we calculate carbon taxes including or excluding existing taxes and subsidies? For example, suppose that a country imposes a $50 carbon tax while maintaining an equivalent subsidy on coal production. Would this be counted as a zero or a $50 carbon tax? Additionally, how would subsidies to zero-carbon fuels, such as wind power, be counted in the analysis?

One approach would be to calculate the net taxation of carbon fuels, including all taxes and subsidies on energy products, but not to go beyond this to indirect, embodied impacts outside exceptional cases. This calculation would require two steps. First, each country would provide a full set of information about taxes and subsidies relating to the energy sector; second, we would need an accepted methodology for combining the different numbers into an overall carbon-tax rate. There would of course be many technical issues, such as how to convert energy taxes into their carbon equivalent. Some of the calculations involve conversion ratios (from coal or oil to carbon equivalent) that underpin any control system. Others require input-output coefficients, which might not be universally available on a timely basis. On the whole, calculations of effective carbon-tax rates are straightforward as long as they do not involve indirect or embodied emissions.

To go beyond first-round calculations to indirect effects would require assumptions about supply and demand elasticities and cross-elasticities, might engender disputes among countries, and should be avoided if possible. The procedure would probably require mechanisms similar to those used in World Trade Organization (WTO) deliberations, where technical experts calculate effective taxes under a set of guidelines that evolve under quasi-legal procedures. Many of these issues are discussed in the literature on ecological taxes.[7]

A Hybrid "Cap-and-Tax" Approach?

Many considerations enter the balance in weighing the relative advantages of prices and quantities in controlling stock public goods. However, we must be realistic about the shortcomings of the price-based approach. It is unfamiliar ground in international environmental agreements. "Tax" is almost a four-letter word. Many people distrust price approaches for environmental policy. Many environmentalists and scientists distrust carbon taxes as an approach to global warming because they do not impose explicit limitations on the growth of emissions or on the concentrations of greenhouse gases. What, they ask, would guarantee that the carbon tax would be set at a level that would prevent "dangerous interferences"? Do carbon emissions, some worry, really respond to prices?

Might the international community fiddle with tax rates, definitions, measurement issues, and participation arguments while the planet burns? These questions have been addressed in this book and other studies, but many people remain unconvinced.

By contrast, quantitative approaches such as cap-and-trade regimes are widely seen as the most realistic approach to slowing global warming. Quantitative restrictions are firmly embedded in the Kyoto Protocol, and most proposals for individual-country policies in the United States and elsewhere, as well as those proposals for deepening the Kyoto Protocol, follow this model. A realistic worry about policies today is not whether they will be cap-and-trade instead of carbon taxes, but whether they will be just plain cap-without-trade. For example, in implementing the Kyoto Protocol, some approaches favor countries doing a substantial fraction of their own mitigation through "domestic implementation" rather than "buying their way out" by purchasing emissions permits from other countries. Even worse, countries might continue to argue and end up doing nothing, as has been the case for the United States up to now.

Given the strong support for cap-and-trade systems among analysts and policymakers, is there a compromise where the strengths of the carbon-tax regime can be crossed with cap-and-trade to get a hardy hybrid? Perhaps the most promising approach would be to supplement a quantitative system with a carbon tax that underpins it—a "cap-and-tax" system. For example, countries could buttress their participation in a cap-and-trade system by imposing a tax of $30 per ton of carbon along with the quantitative restriction. Countries could also put a "safety valve" along with the tax, wherein nations could sell carbon-emissions permits at a multiple of the tax, perhaps at a 50 percent premium, or $45 per ton in this example.[8]

The cap-and-tax system would share some of the strengths and weaknesses of each of the two polar cases. It would not have firm quantitative limits like a pure cap-and-trade system, but the quantitative limits would guide firms and countries and would give some confidence that the climatic targets were being achieved. The hybrid would have some but not all of the advantages of a carbon-tax system. It would have more favorable public-finance characteristics, it would reduce price volatility, it would mitigate the incentives for corruption, and it would help deal with uncertainties. The narrower the band between the tax and the safety-valve price, the more it has the advantages of a carbon tax; the wider the band, the more it has the advantages of a cap-and-trade system.

The coming years will undoubtedly witness intensive negotiations on global warming as the planet warms, the oceans rise, and new ecological and economic impacts are discovered. A dilemma will arise particularly if, as has been suggested earlier, the quantitative approach of the Kyoto Protocol proves to be ineffective and inefficient and no more effective system takes its place. As policymakers search for more effective and efficient ways to slow dangerous climatic change, they should consider the possibility that price-type approaches like harmonized taxes on carbon, or perhaps hybrid approaches like cap-and-tax, could be powerful tools for coordinating policies and slowing global warming.

IX
An Alternative Perspective:
The *Stern Review*

In November 2006, the British government presented a comprehensive new study: *Stern Review on the Economics of Climate Change* (hereafter the *Stern Review*).[1] It painted a dark picture for the globe: "[T]he *Review* estimates that if we don't act, the overall costs and risks of climate change will be equivalent to losing at least 5% of global GDP each year, now and forever. If a wider range of risks and impacts is taken into account, the estimates of damage could rise to 20% of GDP or more. . . . Our actions now and over the coming decades could create risks . . . on a scale similar to those associated with the great wars and the economic depression of the first half of the 20th century."[2]

These results are dramatically different from those of earlier economic models that use the same basic data and analytical structure. One of the major findings in the economics of climate change has been that efficient or "optimal" economic policies to slow climate change involve modest rates of emissions reductions in the near term, followed by sharp reductions in the medium and long terms. We might call this the "climate-policy ramp," in which policies to slow global warming increasingly tighten or ramp up over time.[3]

The findings about the climate-policy ramp have survived the tests of multiple alternative modeling strategies, different climate goals, alternative specifications of the scientific modules, and more than a decade of revisions in integrated assessment models. The logic of the climate-policy ramp is straightforward. In a world where capital is productive, the highest-return investments today are primarily in tangible, technological, and human capital, including research on and development of low-carbon technologies. In the coming decades, damages are predicted to rise relative to output. As that occurs, it becomes efficient to shift investments toward more intensive emissions reductions. The exact mix and timing of emissions reductions depend upon details of the costs, the damages, and the extent to which climate change and damages are nonlinear and irreversible.

There are many perils, costs, and uncertainties—known unknowns as well as unknown unknowns—involved in unchecked climate change.[4] Economic analyses have searched for strategies that will balance the costs of action with the perils of inaction. All economic studies find a case for imposing immediate restraints on GHG emissions, but the difficult questions are how much and how fast. The *Stern Review* is in the tradition of economic cost-benefit analyses, but it reaches strikingly different conclusions from the mainstream economic models.[5] Is this radical revision of global-warming economics warranted? What are the reasons for the difference?[6]

Overview of the Issues

To begin with, the *Stern Review* should be read primarily as a document that is political in nature and has advocacy as its purpose. The review was officially commissioned when British chancellor of the exchequer Gordon Brown "asked Sir Nick Stern to lead a major review of the economics of climate change, to understand more comprehensively the nature of the economic challenges and how they can be met, in the UK and globally."[7] For the most part, the *Stern Review* accurately describes the basic economic questions involved in global warming. However, it tends to emphasize studies and findings that support its policy recommendations, while reports with opposing views about the dangers of global warming are ignored.

Putting this point differently, we might evaluate the *Stern Review* in terms of the ground rules of standard science and economics. The central methodology by which science, including economics, operates is peer review and reproducibility. By contrast, the *Stern Review* was published without an appraisal of methods and assumptions by independent outside experts, and its results cannot be easily reproduced.

These may seem minor points, but they are fundamental for good science. The British government is not infallible in questions of economic and scientific analysis of global warming, any more than it was in its assessment of weapons of mass destruction in Iraq.[8] External review and reproducibility cannot remove all errors, but they are essential for ensuring logical reasoning and a respect for opposing arguments.

A related issue is the difficulty that readers may have in understanding the chain of reasoning. The *Stern Review* was prepared in record time. One of the unfortunate consequences of this haste is that it is a thicket of vaguely connected analyses and reports on the many facets of the economics and science of global warming. Readers will find it difficult to understand or reproduce the line of reasoning that goes from background trends (such as population and technology growth) through emissions and impacts to the finding about the 20 percent cut in consumption, now and forever. The background programs and spreadsheets that underlie the analysis in the *Stern Review* were not published so that analysts could reproduce their results.

Although we can question some of the *Stern Review*'s modeling and economic assumptions, on a more positive note, it makes an important contribution in selecting climate-change policies with an eye to balancing economic priorities with environmental dangers. By linking climate-change policies to both economic and environmental objectives, it has corrected one of the fundamental flaws of the Kyoto Protocol, which had no such linkage.

The next comment concerns the *Stern Review*'s emphasis on the need for increasing the price of carbon emissions. The *Stern Review* summarizes its discussion here as follows: "Creating a transparent and comparable carbon price signal around the world is an urgent challenge for international collective action."[9] In plain English, it is critical to have a harmonized carbon price both to provide incentives for individual firms and households and to stimulate research and development in low-carbon technologies. Carbon prices must be raised to transmit the social costs of GHG emissions to the everyday decisions of billions of firms and people. This simple but inconvenient economic truth is absent from most political discussions of climate-change policy.

But these points are not the nub of the matter. Rather, the *Stern Review*'s radical view of policy stems from an extreme assumption about discounting. Discounting is a factor in climate-change policy—indeed, in all investment decisions—that involves the relative weight of future and present payoffs. At first blush, this area would seem a technicality. Unfortunately, it cannot be buried in a footnote, for discounting is central to the *Stern Review*'s radical position. The *Stern Review* proposes ethical assumptions that produce very low discount rates. Combined with other assumptions, the low discount rate magnifies impacts in the distant future and rationalizes deep cuts in emissions (and indeed in all consumption) today. If we substitute more conventional discount rates used in other global-warming analyses, by governments, by consumers, or by businesses, the *Stern Review*'s dramatic results disappear, and we come back to the climate-policy ramp described earlier. The balance of this chapter focuses on this central issue.

Discounting in Growth and Climate Change

Questions of discounting are central to understanding economic growth theory and policy. They also lie at the heart of the *Stern Review*'s radical view of the grave damages from climate change and the need for immediate steps to sharply reduce GHG. This section reviews some of the core issues, while the next section provides an empirical application of alternative approaches.

ALTERNATIVE DISCOUNT CONCEPTS

Debates about discounting have a long history in economics and public policy. Discounting involves two related and often-confused concepts. One is the idea of a discount rate on goods, which is a positive concept that measures the relative price of goods at different points in time. This is also called the real return on capital, the real interest rate, the opportunity cost of capital, and the real return. The real return measures the yield on investments corrected by the change in the overall price level.

In principle, returns are observable in the marketplace. For example, the real return on 20-year U.S. Treasury securities for 2007 was 2.7 percent per year. The real pretax return on U.S. nonfinancial corporations over the past four decades has averaged about 6.6 percent per year, while the return on U.S. nonfinancial industries over the 1997–2006 period averaged 8.9 percent per year. Estimated real returns on human capital range from 6 percent per year to more than 20 percent per year depending upon the country and the time period. The IPCC Second Assessment Report discussed actual returns and reported real returns on investment ranging from 5 to 26 percent per year.[10] In my empirical work with aggregated and regional models, I generally use a benchmark real return on capital of around 6 percent per year, based on estimates of rates of return from many studies. Since taxes are excluded from this analysis, this is the real discount rate on consumption as well.

The second important discount concept involves the relative weight of the economic welfare of different households or generations over time. This is sometimes called the "pure rate of social time preference," but I will call it the "time discount rate" for brevity. It is calculated as a percent per unit of time, like an interest rate, but refers to the discount in future welfare, not future goods or dollars. A zero time discount rate means that future generations into the indefinite future are treated symmetrically with present generations; a positive

time discount rate means that the welfare of future generations is reduced or "discounted" compared with that of nearer
generations. Philosophers and economists have conducted
vigorous debates about how to apply time discount rates in
areas as diverse as economic growth, climate change, energy
policy, nuclear waste, major infrastructure programs such as
levees, and reparations for slavery.[11]

The sections that follow examine the analytical and
philosophical arguments about intergenerational equity, how
discounting affects the measurement of damages, and the role
of discounting in the economic modeling of climate change,
saving behavior, and behavior under uncertainty.

THE ANALYTICAL BACKGROUND OF OPTIMAL
ECONOMIC GROWTH

Like many other studies of the economics of global warming,
the *Stern Review* puts policy decisions about how to balance
emissions reductions with damages in the framework of economic growth theory. In this framework, the economies of the
world begin with reference paths for consumption, capital,
population, emissions, climate, and so on. Policies change the
trajectory of emissions, GHG concentrations, impacts, and
consumption. Alternative paths of climate policies and consumption are then evaluated by using a social welfare function that ranks the different paths.

The specific approach used by the *Stern Review* to model
the economy and to evaluate the outcomes is the Ramsey-
Koopmans-Cass model of optimal economic growth.[12] In this
theory, a central decision maker desires to maximize a social
welfare function that is the discounted value of the utility of
consumption over some indefinite time period. The economic

units in the economy are generations or cohorts. Economic activity is represented by a single variable, *c(t)*, which can be interpreted as the consumption resources devoted to that generation or cohort on a per capita basis and is discounted to a particular year. This analysis suppresses the details of the decision making of the generation, such as the time profile of consumption, life span, and working and leisure, as well as individual preferences, such as personal risk aversion and time preference, as distinct elements not specifically related to the social choices.

For mathematical convenience, assume that there is a continuum of generations, so that we can analyze the decisions in continuous time. In this framework, as described in Chapter 3, the social welfare function is taken to be an additive separable utilitarian form, $W = \int_0^\infty U[c(t)]e^{-\rho t}dt$. Here, *c(t)* is the per capita consumption of the generation, *U[.]* is the utility function used to compare the relative value of different levels of consumption per generation, and ρ is the time discount rate applied to different generations. For simplicity in the present discussion, I assume a constant population normalized to 1.

We pause for an important cautionary point. It must be emphasized that the variables analyzed here apply to comparisons of the welfare of different generations and not to individual preferences. The individual rates of time preference, risk preference, and utility functions do not, in principle at least, enter into the discussion or arguments at all. An individual may have high time preference, or perhaps double hyperbolic discounting, or negative discounting, but this has no necessary connection with how social decisions weight different generations. Similar cautions apply to the consumption elasticity.

The *Stern Review* argues that it is indefensible to make long-term decisions with a positive time discount rate: "[Our] argument . . . and that of many other economists and philosophers who have examined these long-run, ethical issues, is that [a positive time discount rate] is relevant only to account for the exogenous possibility of extinction."[13] This point is supported by the argument, which is actually neither necessary nor sufficient, that a positive time discount rate would lead societies to ignore large costs that occur in the distant future. The actual time discount rate used in the *Stern Review* is 0.1 percent per year, which is only vaguely justified by estimates of the probability of extinction; for our purposes, it can be treated as near zero.

The *Stern Review* makes the further conventional assumption, as does the DICE model, that the utility function has a constant elasticity of the marginal utility of consumption, α; I call this parameter the "consumption elasticity" for brevity. A constant consumption elasticity implies that the utility function has the form $U[c(t)] = c(t)^{1-\alpha}/(1 - \alpha)$ for $0 \le \alpha \le \infty$.

Optimizing the social welfare function with a constant population and a constant rate of growth of consumption per generation, g^*, yields the standard equation for the relationship between the equilibrium real return on capital, r^*, and the other parameters: $r^* = \rho + \alpha g^*$. We call this the "Ramsey equation," which is embraced by the *Stern Review* as the organizing concept for thinking about intertemporal choices for global-warming policies. The Ramsey equation shows that in a welfare optimum, the rate of return on capital is determined by the generational rate of time preference, the extent to which social policies have aversion to consumption inequality among generations, and the rate of growth of generational consumption. In a growing economy, a high return on capital can arise either from a high time discount rate or high aversion to generational inequality.

How convincing is the *Stern Review*'s argument for its social welfare function, consumption elasticity, and time discount rate? To begin with, there is a major issue concerning the views that are embodied in the social welfare function adopted by the *Stern Review*. It takes the lofty vantage point of the world social planner, perhaps stoking the dying embers of the British Empire, in determining the way in which the world should combat the dangers of global warming. The world, according to Government House utilitarianism,[14] should use the combination of time discounting and consumption elasticity that the *Stern Review*'s authors find persuasive from their ethical vantage point.

I have always found the Government House approach misleading in the context of global warming and particularly as it informs the negotiations of policies among sovereign states. Instead, I would interpret the baseline trajectory, from a conceptual point of view, as one that represents the outcome of market and policy factors as they currently exist. In other words, the DICE model is an attempt to project from a positive perspective the levels and growth of population, output, consumption, saving, interest rates, GHG emissions, climate change, and climatic damages that would occur with no interventions to affect GHG emissions. This approach does not make a case for the social desirability of the distribution of incomes over space or time under existing conditions.

The calculations of changes in world welfare arising from efficient climate-change policies examine potential improvements within the context of the existing distribution of income and investments across space and time. Because this approach relates to discounting, it requires that we look carefully at the returns on alternative investments—at the *real* real interest rate—as the benchmark for climatic investments. The normatively acceptable real interest rates prescribed by philosophers, economists, or the British government are irrelevant to determining the appropriate discount rate to use in the actual financial and capital markets of the United States, China, Brazil, and the rest of the world. When countries weigh their self-interest in international bargains about emissions reductions and burden sharing, they look at the actual gains from bargains, and the returns on these relative to other investments, rather than the gains that would come from a theoretical growth model.

PHILOSOPHICAL QUESTIONS ABOUT THE TIME DISCOUNT RATE

Although I find the ethical reasoning on discount rates in the *Stern Review* largely irrelevant for the actual investments and negotiations about climate change, it is worth considering the arguments for their own merits. At the outset, we should recall the warning that Tjalling Koopmans gave in his pathbreaking analysis of discounting in growth theory: "[T]he problem of optimal growth is too complicated, or at least too unfamiliar, for one to feel comfortable in making an *entirely* a priori choice of [a time discount rate] before one knows the implications of alternative choices."[15] This conclusion applies with even greater force in global-warming models, which have much greater complexity than the simple, deterministic, stationary, two-input models that Koopmans analyzed.

The *Stern Review* argues that fundamental ethics require intergenerational neutrality, represented by a near-zero time

discount rate. The logic behind the *Stern Review*'s social welfare function is not as universal as it would have us believe: it
stems from the British utilitarian tradition with all the controversies and baggage that accompany that philosophical
stance.[16] Quite another ethical stance would be to hold that
each generation should leave at least as much total societal
capital (tangible, natural, human, and technological) as it in-
herited. This would allow a wide array of time discount rates.

A radically different approach would be a Rawlsian perspective that societies should maximize the economic well-
being of the poorest generation. The ethical implication of
this policy would be that current consumption should increase sharply to reflect the projected future improvements in
productivity. An extension of the Rawlsian perspective to uncertainty would be a precautionary (minimax) principle in
which societies maximize minimum consumption along the
riskiest path; this might involve stockpiling vaccines, grain,
oil, and water in contemplation of possible plagues and
famines. Yet further perspectives would consider ecological
values in addition to anthropocentric values. The morals of
major religions—present and future—might clash with the
utilitarian calculus of Ramsey growth theories.

To complicate matters further, note that none of these
approaches touches on the structure of actual intertemporal
decision making because this generation cannot decide for or
tie the hands of future generations.[17] Instead, each generation
is in the position of one member of a relay team, handing off
the baton of capital to the next generation and hoping that
future generations behave sensibly and avoid catastrophic
choices such as dropping or destroying the baton. Moreover,
because we live in an open-economy world of sometimes-
competing and sometimes-cooperating relay teams, we must

consider how the world capital market will equilibrate to the simultaneous relay races, baton dropping, existential wars, and differing norms over space and time.

None of these alternatives is seriously considered by the *Stern Review*, but even without choosing among them, it should be clear that alternative ethical perspectives are possible. Moreover, as I suggest later, alternative perspectives provide vastly different prescriptions about desirable climate-change policies.

REAL INTEREST RATES UNDER ALTERNATIVE CALIBRATIONS OF THE RAMSEY EQUATION

Although time discount rates get most of the headlines, the real return on capital is the variable that drives efficient current emissions reductions. It is the real return on capital that enters into the equality between the marginal consumption cost of emissions reductions today and the discounted marginal consumption benefit of reduced climate damages in the future.

However, in the optimal growth framework, the real return is an endogenous variable that is determined by the Ramsey equation discussed earlier. In equilibrium, the real interest rate depends not only on the time discount rate but also upon a second ethical parameter: the consumption elasticity. A realistic analysis also needs to account for distortions from the tax system, for uncertainties, and for risk premiums on investments, but these complications will be ignored in the present context.[18]

The *Stern Review* assumes that the consumption elasticity is 1, which yields a logarithmic utility function. The elasticity parameter is casually discussed, with no justification in the original report.[19] With an assumed long-run growth of per capita output of 1.3 percent per year and a time discount rate of 0.1 percent per year, this leads to an equilibrium real interest rate of 1.4 percent per year. This rate is apparently used in a partial-equilibrium framework without any reference either to actual rates of return or to the possibility that the economy might not yet have reached the long-run equilibrium.

Even though the real interest rate is crucial to balancing the economic benefits of future damages against present costs of emissions reductions, there is no reference to the decisive role of the real interest rate in the *Stern Review*. However, in calibrating a growth model, the time discount rate and the consumption elasticity cannot be chosen independently if the model is designed to match observable real interest rates and savings rates. To match a real interest rate of, say, 4 percent and a growth in per capita consumption of 1.3 percent per year requires some combination of high time discounting and high consumption elasticity. For example, using the *Stern Review*'s economic growth assumptions, a zero time discount rate requires a consumption elasticity of 3 to produce a 4 percent rate of return. If we adopt the *Stern Review*'s consumption elasticity of 1, then we need a time discount rate of 2.7 percent per year to match the observed rate of return.

The experiments for the DICE-2007 model discussed later in this chapter are slightly different from these equilibrium calculations because of population growth and nonconstant consumption growth, but we can use the equilibrium calculations to give the flavor of the results. In the baseline empirical model, I adopt a time discount rate of 1.5 percent per year with a consumption elasticity of 2. These yield an equilibrium real interest rate of 5.5 percent per year with the consumption growth that is projected over the next century by the DICE-2007 model. It turns out that the calibration of the utility function makes an enormous difference to the results of global-warming models, as I show in the modeling section later.

The *Stern Review*'s approach also has an important implication for consumption and saving.[20] If its philosophy were adopted, it would produce much higher overall saving compared with today. At a first approximation, the *Stern Review*'s assumptions about time discounting and the consumption elasticity would lead to a doubling of the optimal global net savings rate. While this might be worth contemplating, it hardly seems ethically compelling. Global per capita consumption is around $6,600 today. According to the *Stern Review*'s assumptions, this will grow at 1.3 percent per year to around $87,000 in two centuries. If we use these numbers, how persuasive is the ethical stance that we have a duty to reduce current consumption by a substantial amount to improve the welfare of the rich future generations?

A FISCAL-POLICY EXPERIMENT

We can provide an intuitive explanation of the Ramsey analysis by considering a fiscal experiment that asks whether a particular abatement policy improves the consumption possibilities of future generations. Begin with the path of consumption that corresponds to the current state of affairs—one in which there are essentially no policies to reduce GHG emissions; call this path the "baseline" trajectory. Then adopt a set of abatement strategies that correspond to the optimum in the Ramsey growth model. However, along with this optimal abatement strategy, we undertake fiscal tax and transfer policies to maintain the present baseline consumption levels (say, for 50 years). The optimum might have slightly lower consumption in the early years, so the fiscal-policy experiment would involve both abatement and fiscal deficits and debt accumulation for some time, followed by fiscal surpluses and debt repayment later. Call this the "optimal-plus-deficit" strategy. In essence, this alternative keeps consumption the same for the present but rearranges societal investments away from conventional capital (structures, equipment, education, and the like) to investments in abatement of GHG emissions (in climate capital, so to speak).

Assuming that the investments and fiscal policies are efficiently designed so that capital continues to earn its marginal product as measured by the market real return, the optimal-plus-deficit strategy will increase the consumption possibilities of all future generations (those coming after 50 years). In other words, the abatement policies are indeed Pareto-improving. This implies that at some future point, the returns on the investments in climate capital will be reaped, output will rise above the baseline level, and the debt can be repaid.

We can also use this framework to evaluate the *Stern Review*'s very tight emissions-reduction strategy. Consider undertaking its emissions-control strategy and using fiscal policies to keep consumption unchanged for 50 years—that is, the "*Review*-plus-deficit" strategy. Using returns on capital that match estimated market returns, the *Stern Review*'s strategy would leave future generations with less consumption than the optimal-plus-deficit strategy. Indeed, by my calculations, the *Stern Review*'s strategy would leave the future absolutely worse off; it would be Pareto-deteriorating. The *Stern Review*'s approach is inefficient because it invests too much in low-yield abatement strategies too early. After 50 years, conventional capital is much reduced, while climate capital is only slightly increased. The efficient strategy has more investment in conventional capital after the first 50 years and can use those additional resources to invest heavily in climate capital later on.

MEASURING IMPACTS WITH NEAR-ZERO DISCOUNTING

These analytical points are useful in understanding the *Stern Review*'s estimates of the potential damages from climate change. The *Stern Review* concludes, "Putting these . . . factors together would probably increase the cost of climate change to the equivalent of a 20% cut in per-capita consumption, now and forever." This frightening statement suggests that the globe is perilously close to driving off a climatic cliff in the very near future. Faced with this grave prospect, any sensible person would surely reconsider current policies.

A close look reveals that the statement is quite misleading because it employs an unusual definition of consumption losses. When the *Stern Review* says that there are substantial losses "now," it does not mean "today." The measure of consumption used is the "balanced growth equivalents" of consumption, which is essentially a proportional income annuity. With zero discounting, this is the certainty equivalent of the average annual consumption loss over the indefinite future.

In fact, the *Stern Review*'s estimate of the output loss now, as in "today," is essentially zero. Moreover, the projected impacts from climate change occur far in the future. Take as an example the high-climate scenario with catastrophic and nonmarket impacts. For this case, the mean losses are 0.4 percent of world output in 2060, 2.9 percent in 2100, and 13.8 percent in 2200.[21] This is calculated as a loss in "current per capita consumption" of 14.4 percent (see Stern 2007, table 6.1*)*. With even further gloomy adjustments, it becomes the "high+ " case of a "20% cut in per-capita consumption, now and forever."

How do damages that average around 1 percent of output over the next century become a 14.4 percent reduction in consumption now and forever? The answer is that with near-zero discounting, the low damages in the next two centuries get overwhelmed by the long-term average over the many centuries that follow. In fact, if we use the *Stern Review*'s methodology, more than half the estimated damages "now and forever" occur after the year 2800. The damage puzzle is resolved. The large damages from global warming reflect large and speculative damages in the far-distant future magnified into a large current value by a near-zero time discount rate.

A WRINKLE EXPERIMENT

The effect of low discounting can be illustrated by a "wrinkle experiment." Suppose that scientists discover a wrinkle in the climate system that will cause damages equal to 0.1 percent of net consumption starting in 2200 and continuing at that rate forever after. How large a one-time investment would be justified today to remove the wrinkle that starts only after two centuries? If we use the methodology of the *Stern Review,* the answer is that we should pay up to 56 percent of one year's world consumption today to remove the wrinkle.[22] In other words, it is worth a one-time consumption hit of approximately $30,000 billion today to fix a tiny problem that begins in 2200.[23]

It is illuminating to put this point in terms of average consumption levels. Using its growth projections, the *Stern*

Review would justify reducing per capita consumption for one year today from $6,600 to $2,900 in order to prevent a reduction of consumption from $87,000 to $86,900 starting two centuries hence and continuing at that rate forever after. This bizarre result arises because the value of the future consumption stream is so high with near-zero time discounting that we should sacrifice a large fraction of today's income in order to increase a far-future income stream by a very tiny fraction. This is yet another reminder of Koopmans's warning to proceed cautiously in accepting theoretical assumptions about discounting before examining their full consequences.

HAIR TRIGGERS AND UNCERTAINTY

A related feature of the *Stern Review's* near-zero time discount rate is that it puts present decisions on a hair trigger in response to far-future contingencies. Under conventional discounting, contingencies many centuries ahead have a tiny weight in today's decisions. Decisions focus on the near future. With the *Stern Review's* discounting procedure, by contrast, present decisions become extremely sensitive to uncertain events in the distant future.

We saw earlier how an infinitesimal impact on the post-2200 income stream could justify a large consumption sacrifice today. We can use the same example to illustrate how far-future uncertainties are magnified by low discount rates. Suppose that the climatic wrinkle is not a sure thing; rather, there is a 10 percent probability of a wrinkle that would reduce the post-2200 income stream by 0.1 percent. What insurance premium would be justified today to reduce that probability to zero? With conventional discount rates (and, one might say, with common sense), we would ignore any tiny low-probability wrinkle two centuries ahead.

With the *Stern Review*'s near-zero discount rate, offsetting the low-probability wrinkle would be enormously valuable. We would pay an insurance premium today of as much as 8 percent of one year's consumption (about $4 trillion) to remove the year 2200 contingency. If the contingency were thought to occur in 2400 rather than in 2200, the insurance premium would still be 6.5 percent of one year's income. Because the future is so greatly magnified by a near-zero time discount rate, policies for different threshold dates would be virtually identical. Moreover, a small refinement in the probability estimate would trigger a large change in the dollar premium. If someone discovered that the probability of the wrinkle was 15 percent rather than 10 percent, the insurance premium would rise by almost 50 percent (to about $6 trillion).

Although this feature of low discounting might appear benign in climate-change policy, we could imagine other areas where the implications could themselves be dangerous. Imagine the preventive-war strategies that might be devised with low time discount rates. Countries might start wars today because of the possibility of nuclear proliferation a century ahead, or because of a potential adverse shift in the balance of power two centuries ahead, or because of speculative futuristic technologies three centuries ahead. It is not clear how long the globe could survive the calculations and machinations of zero-discount-rate military strategists. This is yet another example of a surprising implication of using a low discount rate.

Alternative Discount Strategies in DICE and the *Stern Review*

The analytical points discussed in earlier sections can usefully be illustrated using empirical models of the economics of global warming. It is virtually impossible for those outside the modeling group to understand the detailed results of the *Stern Review*. It would involve studying the economics and geophysics in several chapters, taking apart a complex analysis (the PAGE [Policy Analysis of the Greenhouse Effect] model), and examining the derivation and implications of each of the economic and scientific judgments. Understanding the analysis is made even more difficult because the detailed calculations behind the *Stern Review* have not been made available.

The alternative approach followed here is to use the DICE-2007 model to understand the logic of the approach in the *Stern Review*. To analyze the approach, I make three runs, which are explained as below:

> Run 1. Optimal climate-change policy in the DICE-2007 model
>
> Run 2. Optimal climate change using the *Stern Review* zero discount rate
>
> Run 3. Optimal climate change using a zero discount rate and a recalibrated consumption elasticity

Note that these runs take a different approach from that of earlier chapters. The earlier estimates used a consistent objective function in analyzing all policies. In this chapter, we investigate the impact of alternative objective functions.

Run 1 calculates the optimal climate-change policy in the DICE-2007 model. This run takes the DICE-2007 model and calculates the optimal trajectory of climate-change policies as described in earlier chapters. Run 1 (the optimal run of earlier chapters) has an optimal carbon price of $42 per ton of carbon in 2015, rising over time to $95 in 2050 and to $207 in 2100 (all data are in 2005 U.S. dollars). The social cost of carbon without emissions restraints is $28 per ton of carbon in 2005. The optimal rate of emissions reduction is 16 percent in 2015, 25 percent in 2050, and 42 percent in 2100. This optimized path leads to a projected global temperature increase from 1900 to 2100 of 2.8°C.

The standard-DICE-model results just discussed are radically different from those in the *Stern Review*. The *Stern Review* estimates that the current social cost of carbon in the uncontrolled regime is $350 per ton of carbon in 2005 prices.[24] This number is more than 10 times the DICE-model result. It seems likely that the major reason for the *Stern Review*'s sharp emissions reductions and high social cost of carbon is the low time discount rate.

I therefore calculated Run 2, optimal climate change using the *Stern Review* zero discount rate. The assumptions are the same as in Run 1 except that the time discount rate is changed to 0.1 percent per year and the consumption elasticity is changed to 1. This dramatically changes the trajectory of climate-change policy. The 2015 optimal carbon price in the DICE model rises from $42 per ton in Run 1 to $348 per ton in Run 2. Recommended emissions reductions in Run 2 are much larger—with emissions reductions of 51 percent in 2025—because future damages are in effect treated as though they were occurring today. So Run 2 confirms the intuition that a low real return on capital leads to a very high initial carbon price and very sharp initial emissions reductions. The climate-policy ramp flattens out.

One of the problems with Run 2 is that it generates real returns that are too low and savings rates that are too high compared with actual market data. We correct this with Run

3, optimal climate change using a zero discount rate and a recalibrated consumption elasticity. This run draws on the Ramsey equation; it keeps the near-zero time discount rate and calibrates the consumption elasticity to match observable variables. This calibration yields parameters of $\rho = 0.1$ percent per year and $\alpha = 3$. The calibration produces a real return on capital for the first eight periods of 5.2 percent per year for Run 3, compared with an average for Run 1 of 5.3 percent per year. Run 2 (the *Stern Review* run) has a real return of 1.9 percent per year over the period.

Run 3 looks very similar to Run 1, which is the standard DICE-2007 model's optimal policy. The optimal carbon price for Run 3 in 2015 is $43, which is slightly above Run 1's $42 per ton of carbon. The recalibrated run looks nothing like Run 2, which reflects the *Stern Review*'s assumptions. How can it be that Run 3, with a near-zero time discount rate, looks so much like Run 1? The reason is that Run 3 maintains a structure with a high return on capital. This calibration removes, for the near term at least, the cost-benefit dilemmas as well as the savings and uncertainty problems discussed earlier.

Figures 9-1 and 9-2 show the time paths of optimal carbon taxes and rates of return on capital under the three runs examined here. These figures illustrate the point that it is not the time discount rate itself that determines the high carbon tax in the *Stern Review* runs, but the combination of the time discount rate and the consumption elasticity as they work through the rate of return on capital.

These experiments highlight that the central difference between the *Stern Review* and many other economic models lies in the implicit real return on capital embedded in the model. The *Stern Review*'s calibration gives too low a rate

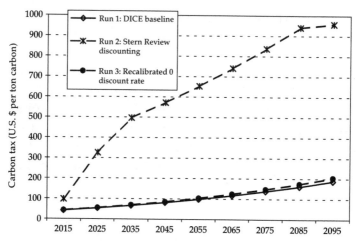

Figure 9-1. Optimal carbon tax in three alternative runs for the *Stern Review* analysis. The calculated optimal carbon tax, or the price that equilibrates the marginal cost of damages with the marginal cost of emissions, in the different runs. The runs are explained in the text. These numbers are slightly below the estimated social cost of carbon for the uncontrolled runs. Values are prices per ton of carbon in 2005 international U.S. dollars.

of return and too high a savings rate compared with actual macroeconomic data. If the model is designed to fit current market data, then the modeler has only one and not two degrees of freedom in choosing the time discount rate and the consumption elasticity. The *Stern Review* seems to have become lost in the discounting trees and failed to see the capital market forest by overlooking the constraints on the two normative parameters.

Since this analysis was first undertaken, similar results have been found by other modelers. A particularly enlightening set of runs was made by Chris Hope, who is the designer of

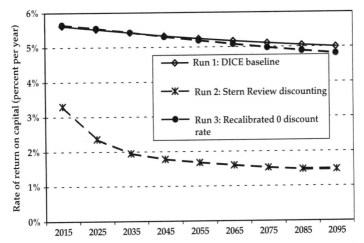

Figure 9-2. Rate of return on capital in alternative runs. The marginal product of capital in the different runs for the analysis of the approach of the *Stern Review*. Conceptually, the return is the discount rate on consumption from one period to the next. The model contains no inflation, risk, or taxes. The figure is the estimated geometric average real return from the date shown to the next date.

the PAGE model that was used for some economic modeling runs in the *Stern Review*. Hope attempted to replicate the *Stern Review*'s results in his own model. He found that when he substituted the assumptions and discount rates that were normally used in the PAGE model, the mean social cost of carbon was only $43 per ton of carbon. Simply substituting a discount rate of 0.1 percent per year into the PAGE model raises the mean social cost of carbon from $43 per ton of carbon to $364 per ton of carbon, which is close to the ratio found here.[25] A study by Sergey Mityakov, using yet another calibrated model of the economics of global warming, finds that the *Stern Review*'s discounting assumptions raise the present value of damages by a factor of 8 to 16, depending upon which baseline discount rate is used.[26]

What should the prudent reader conclude from all this? Global warming is a complex phenomenon, and there are many perspectives that can help illuminate the issues. Sensible decision making requires a robust set of alternative scenarios and sensitivity analyses to determine whether some rabbit has in the dead of night jumped into the hat and is responsible for some unusual results. One of the major flaws in the *Stern Review* is the absence of just such robust analyses.

Summary Verdict

How much and how fast should the globe reduce GHG emissions? How should nations balance the costs of these reductions against the damages and dangers of climate change? The *Stern Review* answers these questions clearly and unambiguously: We need urgent, sharp, and immediate reductions in GHG emissions.

I am reminded of President Harry Truman's complaint that his economists would always say, on the one hand this and on the other hand that. He wanted a one-handed economist. The *Stern Review* is a president's or a prime minister's dream come true. It provides decisive answers instead of the dreaded conjectures, contingencies, and qualifications. However, a closer look reveals that there is indeed another hand to these answers. The *Stern Review*'s radical revision of the economics of climate change does not arise from any new economics, science, or modeling. Rather, it depends decisively on the assumption of a near-zero time discount rate combined with a specific utility function. The *Stern Review*'s unambiguous conclusions about the need for extreme immediate action will not survive the substitution of assumptions that are more consistent with today's market real interest and savings rates. Hence the central questions about global-warming policy—how much, how fast, and how costly—remain open. The *Stern Review* does not provide useful answers to these fundamental questions.

X
Summary and Conclusions

This book presents the results of the DICE-2007 model, which is a complete revision of earlier models of the economics of global warming. The model is a globally aggregated model that incorporates simplified representations of the major elements involved in analyzing the problems associated with climate change. The major feature of the DICE model is that it allows us to analyze in a simplified and transparent fashion the economic and environmental impacts of alternative policies, including one with no controls, an economic optimum, and ones targeted on climatic constraints, as well as ones that derive from current policies such as the Kyoto Protocol. We conclude this book with some reservations and summary conclusions.

Reservations

We begin with some reservations that should be kept in mind in weighing the results of this book. These reservations are in addition to the contentious issues discussed in Chapter 3. The first reservation is that the structure, equations, data, and parameters of the model all have major uncertain elements. Virtually none of the major components is completely understood. Moreover, because the model embodies long-term projections of poorly understood phenomena, the results should be viewed as having growing error bounds the further the projections move into the future. As an example, the temperature projections indicate an uncertainty range (roughly the middle two-thirds of the distribution) of 1.9 to 4.0°C for 2100.

The impact of uncertainties on policies is not obvious. The common presumption is that uncertainty would lead to tighter restrictions on carbon emissions or higher carbon taxes. This, however, is not necessarily correct. If the uncertainties come primarily from changes in productivity, then the presence of uncertainty might lead to lower optimal carbon taxes. Moreover, sensible policies will depend upon the time path of the resolution of the uncertainties; a more rapid resolution of uncertainty implies that it may be beneficial to impose less costly restraints until the exact nature of future consequences is revealed. One preliminary finding of the uncertainty analysis in this book is that the best-guess or certainty-equivalent policy differs little from the expected-value policy.

A second reservation, related to the first, is that the DICE model is but one approach to understanding the economic and policy issues involved in global warming. It embodies the modeling philosophy and the analytical and empirical proclivities and biases of its author. Other models provide different perspectives and important insights that cannot be obtained from this approach. Particularly important are issues such as aggregation over space and time, distributional issues over rich and poor generations and nations, dynamics, atmospheric chemistry, regional detail in geophysical sciences, fixity of capital stocks, political rigidities, and bargaining questions in international agreements. No medicine can effectively cure all diseases, and no model can accurately answer all questions.

A third major reservation is that the DICE model contains highly simplified representations of the major relationships among emissions, concentrations, climate change, the costs of emissions reductions, and the impacts of climate change. Much regional detail is hidden or lost in the aggregation, and some of the trade-offs involved, particularly between rich and poor regions, cannot be explored.

The use of highly aggregated relationships is motivated by one primary concern. The relationships among the different parts of the system are extremely complex, particularly because they involve long time dynamics. It is useful, therefore, to work with a model that is as simple and as transparent as possible. Complex systems cannot be easily understood, and strange behavior may well arise because of the interaction of complex nonlinear relationships. To include more sectors of the economy, more layers of the ocean, more greenhouse gases, more energy resources, more layers of production functions, or multiple regions would reduce transparency, hinder use of the model, and impair its ability to conduct sensitivity analyses. Apologies are extended to those who feel that their discipline has been grossly oversimplified. Along with the apologies go invitations to help improve our understanding by providing better parsimonious representations of the crucial geophysical or economic processes. In modeling, small is genuinely beautiful.

Major Results and Conclusions

This book contains many results that have been discussed along the way. In this section, I highlight 10 major conclusions.

The first major point is that an ideal and efficient climate-change policy would be relatively inexpensive and would have a substantial impact on long-run climate change. This policy, which we have labeled the "optimal" one, sets emissions reductions to maximize the economic welfare of humans. The net present-value benefit of the optimal policy is $3 trillion. Our estimate is that the present value of global abatement costs for the optimal policy would be around $2 trillion, which is 0.1 percent of discounted world income. (Recall that all dollar values in the text, tables, and graphs are in 2005 U.S. dollars and are measured in purchasing-power-parity exchange rates.)

The optimal policy reduces the global temperature rise relative to 1900 to 2.6°C in 2100 and to 3.4°C in 2200. If concentration or temperature limits are added to the economic optimum, the additional cost is relatively modest for all but the most ambitious targets. For example, imposing a constraint in which CO_2 concentrations are limited to a doubling of preindustrial levels has an additional present-value cost of $0.4 trillion, while limiting global temperature increases to 2.5°C has an additional present-value cost of $1.1 trillion over the optimum.

Note that although the net impact of policies is relatively small, the total discounted climatic damages are large. We estimate that the present value of climatic damages in the base-line (uncontrolled) case is $22.6 trillion, compared with $17.3 trillion in the optimal case.

The second point refers to findings about the social cost of carbon (SCC) along with carbon taxes or prices. Our estimate, shown in Table 5-1, is that the SCC in the baseline case is about $28 per metric ton of carbon in 2005. (Often, prices are quoted in terms of prices for carbon dioxide, which are smaller by a factor of 3.67, so the current SCC is $7.40 per ton of CO_2.) This figure is slightly higher than the optimal carbon tax, which is estimated to be $27 per ton of carbon in 2005.

These numbers are the most informative indicator of the optimal tightness of climate-change policies. The optimal carbon tax indicates the level of restraint on carbon emissions that would need to be imposed in order to put the globe on the economically optimal path—the path on which incremental costs and benefits are balanced. The baseline SCC indicates the maximum value that any efficient emissions-control program should take. An efficient partial program (say, one with less than complete participation) might have a carbon price above the optimal price, but it would never be above the no-controls SCC.

The SCCs with the intermediate climatic objectives are slightly higher than those of the baseline or optimal programs because they implicitly assume very high costs at the thresholds. For example, the initial SCC with a limit of doubling CO_2 concentrations is $29.20 per ton of carbon, compared with $28.10 per ton of carbon for the baseline. The carbon taxes that would apply to the climatic limits, except for the very stringent case, are close to those of the economic optimum. For example, the 2010 carbon prices associated with the CO_2-doubling and 2.5°C cases are $40 and $42 per ton of carbon, respectively, compared with $34 per ton for the optimum without limits.

This book also shows that the trajectory of optimal carbon prices should rise sharply over the coming decades to reflect rising damages and the need for increasingly tight restraints. For example, in the optimal trajectory, the carbon price would rise to $95 per ton of carbon by 2050 and to $202 per ton of carbon by 2100. The ultimate limit of the carbon price would be determined by the cost at which the backstop technology (a technology that provides superabundant supplies of zero-carbon fuel substitutes for all uses) would become available. Note as well that the climatic-limit cases show steeper increases in the carbon price depending upon the precise target chosen.

The third point concerns the need for cost-effective policies (or, conversely, the need to avoid inefficient policies). The results cited in the first two summary points assume that the policies are efficiently deployed. This means that carbon prices are harmonized across sectors and countries, that there are no exemptions or favored sectors, and that the time path of carbon prices is correctly chosen. All of these are unrealistic in the world we know today. For example, in the Kyoto Protocol, carbon prices are different across countries (from high to zero); within covered countries, some sectors are favored; and there is no mechanism to guarantee an efficient allocation over time.

As an example of highly inefficient strategies, we can look at the results for the Kyoto Protocol without the United States. In this case, because the regime is so minimal and distorted, the present value of the damages is only $0.12 trillion less than the baseline, while the abatement costs are $0.07 trillion higher. This estimate assumes that the policy is efficiently implemented within the Protocol region, which is clearly not the case.

The ambitious policies proposed in the Stern and Gore regimes have the opposite problem. They are inefficient because they impose too-large emissions reductions in the short run. In other words, they do not take into account that an efficient emissions-control policy has an upward-sloping ramp, as shown in Figures 5-4 and 5-5. Because the initial emissions reductions are so sharp in the ambitious proposals, they impose much higher costs to attain the same environmental objective.

Moreover, the results here incorporate an estimate of the importance of participation for economic efficiency. Complete participation is important because the cost function for abatement appears to be highly convex. We preliminarily estimate that a participation rate of 50 percent instead of 100 percent will impose a cost penalty on abatement of 250 percent.

Similar issues arise for policies that use technological standards in place of generalized market mechanisms. Two prominent proposals are to ban coal-fired power plants and to raise sharply fuel-economy standards for automobiles. Although both of these industries will require major adjustments if tight restraints are imposed on emissions, technology standards are blunt and inefficient instruments. Calculations of the carbon-tax equivalent of some fuel-economy proposals indicate that they are far above the optimal carbon tax and thereby impose larger costs than necessary to meet the same objectives.

We can also think of participation in terms of whether the entire economy is covered by an emissions-control strategy. Many policies focus on small slices of the economy, such as fuel-economy standards for the automobile industry. The high costs of limited participation apply with equal force here. For example, if half the economy with average emissions intensities is exempted because of political concerns with, say, farmers, the poor, labor unions, powerful lobbies, or international competitiveness, then the cost of attaining a climatic objective will also have a cost penalty of 250 percent. The concerns about participation apply within, as well as across, countries.

The fourth point concerns the DICE-model projections for GHG emissions and climate change. The DICE projections for emissions show a different pattern from that of many of the projections used by the IPCC. As shown in Figure 3-2, the DICE-model baseline CO_2 emissions are at the low end of the SRES projections through 2030. However, after that time, the SRES scenarios tend to stagnate, while the DICE-model projections under a baseline, no-controls strategy continue to grow rapidly.

The DICE baseline temperature projections are in the lower-middle end of the projections analyzed in the IPCC's Fourth Assessment Report. The IPCC Fourth Assessment Report gives a best estimate of the global mean temperature increase of between 1.8 and 4.0°C from 1980–1999 to 2090–2099. The DICE baseline yields a global mean temperature increase of 2.2°C over this same period.[1]

The fifth point is that the economic benefits of a low-cost and environmentally benign backstop technology are huge in terms of net impacts, averted costs, averted damages, and benefit-cost ratio. We estimate that a low-cost technological solution would have a net present value of around $17 trillion.

The sixth point involves an analysis of the Kyoto Protocol. The analyses in this book and several earlier studies indicate that the current Kyoto Protocol is seriously flawed both in its environmental rationale and in its economic impacts. The approach of freezing emissions for a subgroup of countries is not related to a particular goal for concentrations, temperature, or damages. As shown in Table 5-3, the different versions of the Kyoto Protocol all pass a cost-benefit test.

However, their net benefits are very small relative to other policies. For example, as shown in Table 5-1, the current Kyoto Protocol (without the United States) has net benefits of around $0.15 trillion, compared with $3.4 trillion for the efficient policy. Moreover, once the inefficiencies of the different versions of the Protocol are included, they are unlikely to pass even the minimal cost-benefit test used here.

A different and more optimistic interpretation of the Kyoto Protocol is that it is an awkward first step on the road to a more efficient international agreement on climate change. The fact that the initial emissions reductions are low is not inconsistent with the results of this book, although the implementation is extremely inefficient. If we view the Kyoto glass as one-quarter full rather than three-quarters empty, then there are important changes that need to be incorporated to improve its performance.

The seventh conclusion involves what we have called the "ambitious proposals"—proposals associated with the *Stern Review*, proposals of former Vice President Gore, and a recent proposal from the German government. These proposals are tilted toward early emissions reductions. Although the *Stern Review* had no explicit target, it suggested that an 85 percent global emissions reduction would be necessary to meet its 450 ppm target (see Stern 2007, figure 8.4, although there is some ambiguity between CO_2 concentrations and CO_2-equivalent concentrations). The 2007 Gore proposal for the United States—a 90 percent reduction in CO_2 emissions below current levels—is even sharper. Similarly ambitious was the 2007 German proposal to limit global CO_2 emissions to 50 percent of 1990 levels by 2050.

Clearly, meeting these ambitious objectives would require sharp emissions reductions, but the timing induced by excessively early reductions makes the policies much more expensive than necessary. For example, the Gore and Stern proposals have net costs of $17 trillion to $22 trillion relative to no controls; they are more costly than doing nothing today. The emissions target of the German proposal is close to that of the *Stern Review*'s analysis, and the cost penalty is likely to be similar. This conclusion does not mean that doing nothing forever is preferable to these proposals. Rather, it implies that it is not economically advantageous to undertake sharp emissions reductions (such as reducing emissions 80 or 90 percent) within the next two or three decades.

Eighth, we have undertaken a preliminary uncertainty analysis. An important application of the uncertainty runs investigates the question of the risk properties of high-climate-change outcomes. Should economies be risk averse to outcomes where climate change is at the high end? The modern theory of risk and insurance holds that the risk premium on different outcomes is determined by the correlation of a risk with consumption in different states of the world. Our calculations have uncovered a major paradox: High-climate-change outcomes, as measured by temperature change, are positively correlated with consumption. This leads to the paradoxical result that there is actually a negative risk premium on high-climate-change states. This paradox arises because in our calculations the uncertainty about total factor productivity growth (which is positively correlated with consumption) outweighs the uncertainties of the climate system and the damage function (which are negatively correlated with consumption).

Ninth, the size and scope of the interventions in the energy market from the climate policies analyzed here should not be underestimated. Figure 5-11 shows carbon revenue transfers as a percentage of total consumption for different policies and periods. The revenue transfers are the total dollars transferred from consumers to producers (if permits are allocated to producers) or to governments (if constraints are imposed through efficient carbon taxes). The redistribution of income is a substantial fraction of world consumption, particularly for the ambitious plans. For these, transfers or taxes would be about 2 percent of world consumption in the near term. For example, an emissions reduction of 50 percent in 2015 is estimated to require a carbon tax of around $300 per ton of carbon, which would yield a total transfer of around $1,500 trillion globally from consumers. Although such amounts are not unheard of in extreme fiscal circumstances such as wartime, they require a fiscal mobilization not normally seen. The transfers in the optimal or climate-limit programs rise gradually to around 1 percent of consumption, which is itself a major change in fiscal structure. Given the squawks that often arise from relatively small tax or price increases, even a modest program like the economic optimum is likely to prove politically arduous.

As a final point, we have examined the relative advantages of price-type approaches like carbon taxes and quantity-type approaches such as are used in the Kyoto Protocol. Many considerations enter into the balance. One advantage of price-type approaches is that they can more easily and flexibly integrate the economic costs and benefits of emissions reductions, whereas the approach in the Kyoto Protocol has no discernible connection with ultimate environmental or economic goals. This advantage is emphatically reinforced by the large uncertainties and evolving scientific knowledge in this area. Emissions taxes are more efficient in the face of massive uncertainties because of the relative linearity of the benefits compared with the costs. A related point is that quantitative limits will produce high volatility in the market price of carbon under an emissions-targeting approach. In addition, a tax approach can capture the revenues more easily than quantitative approaches, and a price-type approach will therefore cause fewer additional tax distortions. The tax approach also provides less opportunity for corruption and financial finagling than quantitative limits because the tax approach creates no artificial scarcities to encourage rent-seeking behavior.

Carbon taxes appear to be disadvantageous because they do not impose hard constraints on emissions, concentrations, or temperature change. However, this is largely an illusory disadvantage. There are great uncertainties about what emissions or concentrations or temperature would actually lead to the dangerous interferences—or even if there are dangerous interferences. The key question is: Which of the policy approaches would allow flexibility in changing policies as new evidence becomes available? Would it would prove easier to make periodic large adjustments to incorrectly set harmonized carbon taxes or to incorrectly negotiated emissions limits? The relative flexibility of these mechanisms is an open research question.

We suggest that a hybrid approach, which we call "cap-and-tax," might combine the strengths of both quantity and price approaches. An example of a hybrid plan would be a traditional cap-and-trade system combined with a base carbon tax and a safety valve available at a penalty price. For example, the initial carbon tax might be $30 per ton of carbon, with safety-valve purchases of additional permits available at a 50 percent premium.

The major message about policy instruments is the following: As policymakers search for more effective and efficient

.

ways to slow dangerous climatic change, they should consider the possibility that price-type approaches like harmonized taxes on carbon are powerful tools for coordinating policies and slowing global warming.

The summary message of this book is that climate change is a complex phenomenon, subject to great uncertainty, and changes in our knowledge occur virtually daily. Climate change is unlikely to be catastrophic in the near term, but it has the potential for serious damages in the long run. There are big economic stakes in designing efficient approaches. The total discounted economic damages with no abatement are on the order of $23 trillion. These damages can be significantly reduced by well-designed policies, but poorly designed ones, like the current Kyoto Protocol, are unlikely to make a dent in the damages, will have substantial costs, and may cool enthusiasm for more efficient approaches. Similarly, overly ambitious projects are likely to be full of exemptions, loopholes, and compromises and may cause more economic damage than benefit.

In the author's view, the best approach is one that gradually introduces restraints on carbon emissions. One particularly efficient approach is internationally harmonized carbon taxes—ones that quickly become global and universal in scope and harmonized in effect. A sure and steady increase in harmonized carbon taxes may not have the swashbuckling romance of a crash program, but it is also less likely to be smashed on the rocks of political opposition and compromise. Slow, steady, universal, predictable, and boring—these are probably the secrets for successful policies to combat global warming.

Appendix: Equations of the DICE-2007 Model

This appendix presents the major equations in the DICE-2007 model. We omit unimportant equations such as initial conditions. For the full set of equations, see the GAMS program available online at http://www.econ.yale.edu/~nordhaus/homepage/DICE2007.htm.

Model Equations

(A.1) $\quad W = \displaystyle\sum_{t=1}^{Tmax} u[c(t), L(t)]R(t)$

(A.2) $\quad R(t) = (1 + \rho)^{-t}$

(A.3) $\quad U[c(t), L(t)] = L(t)[c(t)^{1-\alpha}/(1 - \alpha)]$

(A.4) $\quad Q(t) = \Omega(t)[1 - \Lambda(t)]A(t)K(t)^{\gamma}L(t)^{1-\gamma}$

(A.5) $\quad \Omega(t) = 1/[1 + \psi_1 T_{AT}(t) + \psi_2 T_{AT}(t)^2]$

(A.6) $\quad \Lambda(t) = \pi(t)\theta_1(t)\mu(t)^{\theta_2}$

(A.7) $Q(t) = C(t) + I(t)$

(A.8) $c(t) = C(t)/L(t)$

(A.9) $K(t) = I(t) + (1 - \delta_K)K(t-1)$

(A.10) $E_{Ind}(t) = \sigma(t)[1 - \mu(t)]A(t)K(t)^\gamma L(t)^{1-\gamma}$

(A.11) $CCum \geq \sum_{t=0}^{Tmax} E_{Ind}(t)$

(A.12) $E(t) = E_{Ind}(t) + E_{Land}(t)$

(A.13) $M_{AT}(t) = E(t) + \phi_{11}M_{AT}(t-1) + \phi_{21}M_{UP}(t-1)$

(A.14) $M_{UP}(t) = \phi_{12}M_{AT}(t-1) + \phi_{22}M_{UP}(t-1) + \phi_{32}M_{LO}(t-1)$

(A.15) $M_{LO}(t) = \phi_{23}M_{UP}(t-1) + \phi_{33}M_{LO}(t-1)$

(A.16) $F(t) = \eta\{log_2[M_{AT}(t)/M_{AT}(1750)]\} + F_{EX}(t)$

(A.17) $T_{AT}(t) = T_{AT}(t-1) + \xi_1\{F(t) - \xi_2 T_{AT}(t-1) - \xi_3[T_{AT}(t-1) - T_{LO}(t-1)]\}$

(A.18) $T_{LO}(t) = T_{LO}(t-1) + \xi_4\{T_{AT}(t-1) - T_{LO}(t-1)]\}$

(A.19) $\pi(t) = \varphi(t)^{1-\theta_2}$

Variable Definitions and Units (Endogenous Variables Marked with Asterisks)

$A(t)$ = total factor productivity (productivity units)

*$c(t)$ = capita consumption of goods and services (2005 U.S. dollars per person)

*$C(t)$ = consumption of goods and services (trillions of 2005 U.S. dollars)

$E_{Land}(t)$ = emissions of carbon from land use (billions of metric tons of carbon per period)

$^{\star}E_{Ind}(t)$ = industrial carbon emissions (billions of metric tons of carbon per period)

$^{\star}E(t)$ = total carbon emissions (billions of metric tons of carbon per period)

$^{\star}F(t)$, $F_{EX}(t)$ = total and exogenous radiative forcing (watts per square meter from 1900)

$^{\star}I(t)$ = investment (trillions of 2005 U.S. dollars)

$^{\star}K(t)$ = capital stock (trillions of 2005 U.S. dollars)

$L(t)$ = population and labor inputs (millions)

$^{\star}M_{AT}(t)$, $M_{UP}(t)$, $M_{LO}(t)$ = mass of carbon in reservoir for atmosphere, upper oceans, and lower oceans (billions of metric tons of carbon, beginning of period)

$^{\star}Q(t)$ = net output of goods and services, net of abatement and damages (trillions of 2005 U.S. dollars)

t = time (decades from 2001–2010, 2011–2020, . . .)

$^{\star}T_{AT}(t)$, $T_{LO}(t)$ = global mean surface temperature and temperature of lower oceans (°C increase from 1900)

$^{\star}U[c(t),\ L(t)]$ = instantaneous utility function (utility per period)

$^{\star}W$ = objective function in present value of utility (utility units)

$^{\star}\Lambda(t)$ = abatement-cost function (abatement costs as fraction of world output)

$^{\star}\mu(t)$ = emissions-control rate (fraction of uncontrolled emissions)

$^{\star}\Omega(t)$ = damage function (climate damages as fraction of world output)

$\star \varphi(t)$ = participation rate (fraction of emissions included in policy)

$\star \pi(t)$ = participation cost markup (abatement cost with incomplete participation as fraction of abatement cost with complete participation)

$\star \sigma(t)$ = ratio of uncontrolled industrial emissions to output (metric tons of carbon per output in 2005 prices)

Parameters

α = elasticity of marginal utility of consumption (pure number)

$CCum$ = maximum consumption of fossil fuels (billions of metric tons of carbon)

γ = elasticity of output with respect to capital (pure number)

δ_k = rate of depreciation of capital (per period)

$R(t)$ = social time preference discount factor (per time period)

$Tmax$ = length of estimate period for model (60 periods = 600 years)

η = temperature-forcing parameter (°C per watts per meter squared)

$\phi_{11}, \phi_{12}, \phi_{21}, \phi_{22}, \phi_{23}, \phi_{32}, \phi_{33}$ = parameters of the carbon cycle (flows per period)

ψ_1, ψ_2 = parameters of damage function

ρ = pure rate of social time preference (per unit time)

$\theta_1(t), \theta_2$ = parameters of the abatement-cost function
$\xi_1, \xi_2, \xi_3, \xi_4$ = parameters of climate equations (flows per period)

Note on Time Period

The current model runs on 10-year time-steps. Variables are generally defined as flow per year, but some variables are in flow per decade. The transition parameters are generally defined per decade. Users should check the GAMS program to determine the exact definition of the time-steps.

Notes

Introduction

1. The earlier versions were published in a series of studies and books. The central descriptions were Nordhaus 1979, Nordhaus and Yohe 1983, Nordhaus 1994, and Nordhaus and Boyer 2000.

Chapter II
Background and Description of the DICE Model

1. Extensive discussions on this subject are contained in reports by the IPCC, especially IPCC 2007b.

2. See European Commission 2006 and Klepner and Peterson 2005. For analysis of the structure and effects, see Ellerman and Buchner 2007, Convery and Redmond 2007, and Kruger, Oates, and Pizer 2007.

3. This was projected in early studies by Nordhaus and Boyer 1999, Nordhaus 2001, Manne and Richels 1999, and MacCracken et al. 1999. The same basic results have been confirmed in this book, as discussed in Chapter 5.

4. For reference purposes, this study uses the DICE-2007.delta.v8 version. Details on the revisions, with sources and methods, are provided in a document available at http://www.econ.yale.edu/~nordhaus/homepage/DICE2007.htm.

Chapter III
Derivation of the Equations of the DICE-2007 Model

1. United Nations, Department of Social and Economic Affairs 2004 shows the U.N. series, while the new IIASA projections were made available by Lutz 2007.

2. International Monetary Fund 2006. We apply a downward adjustment of 35 percent for China to reflect the likelihood that the Chinese PPP GDP is overestimated.

3. The basic description of the damages model is in Nordhaus and Boyer 2000.

4. The abatement-cost function is calibrated to a survey of estimates of abatement-cost functions, as well as estimates made by the MiniCam (Edmonds 2007). See the discussion later in this chapter for a further description.

5. MAGICC 2007. According to results reported in IPCC 2007b, p. 809, the estimated temperature sensitivity of the MAGICC model with the standard carbon cycle is slightly higher than the mean for the Atmosphere-Ocean General Circulation Models (AOGCMs) for all the SRES scenarios. For the A2 scenario, for example, the reported global temperature increase in 2090 to 2099 relative to the 1980 to 1999 average is about 0.2°C higher for MAGICC than the mean for the AOGCMs. It is unclear, however, whether the software available for this book corresponds exactly to that used for the IPCC calculations.

6. MAGICC 2007. For details on the calibration, see "Accompanying Notes and Documentation on Development of DICE-2007 Model" (Nordhaus 2007a).

7. See Brooke et al. 2005.

8. Details on the revisions with sources and methods are contained in "Accompanying Notes and Documentation on Development of DICE-2007 Model" (Nordhaus 2007a).

9. A full discussion of the issues involved in the use of purchasing-power-parity versus market exchange rates is contained in Nordhaus 2007b.

10. See IPCC 2001b for the IPCC study. I am grateful to Jeff Sachs for pointing out this problem, and to Jae Edmonds and John Weyant for assistance in calibrating the new function.

11. IPCC 1996.

12. Manne and Richels 1992, Nordhaus and Popp 1997, Nordhaus and Boyer 2000, Nordhaus 1994, Peck and Teisberg 1993, Hope 2006, and Webster 2002.

Chapter IV
Alternative Policies for Global Warming

1. Twenty-five periods is an arbitrary length chosen to minimize computational problems. There is essentially no difference if the no-controls period is 250 years or longer. For example, using a no-controls period of 350 years has an additional net present-value cost of $4 billion (0.0002 percent of discounted income), and the initial value of the Hotelling rents is identical to the fourth significant digit.

2. See United Nations 2007.

3. See Oppenheimer 1998 and Oppenheimer and Alley 2004.

4. See, for example, Keller et al. 2005.

5. For a recent discussion, see Füssel et al. 2003, which also calculates emissions trajectories that would keep climate safely beneath a temperature trajectory that might trigger changes in thermohaline circulation. All runs of DICE-2007 are well below the trigger trajectory.

6. See Wigley, Richels, and Edmonds 1996.

7. The analysis of participation is contained in Chapter 6.

8. See the articles in Weyant and Hill 1999.

9. See Stern 2007, as well as Cline 1992.

10. This was widely reported, for example, in *Congressional Quarterly* 2007.

11. Gore 2007.

12. National Academy of Sciences 1992, p. 460. The National Academy report describes a number of options that provide the theoretical capability of unlimited offsets to the radiative effects of GHGs at a cost of less than $1 per ton of carbon (see National Academy of Sciences 1992, chap. 28).

13. An excellent survey is contained in Keith 2000. An advocacy document is contained in Teller, Wood, and Hyde 1997. See Govindasamy, Caldeira, and Duffy 2003 for some geophysical considerations.

Chapter V
Results of the DICE-2007 Model Runs

1. See the articles in Weyant and Hill 1999.

2. "Peer-reviewed estimates of the SCC for 2005 have an average value of US $43 per tonne of carbon (tC) (i.e., US $12 per tonne of carbon dioxide) but the range around, this mean is large. For example, in a survey

of 100 estimates, the values ran from US $ −10 per tonne of carbon (US $ −3 per tonne of carbon dioxide) up to US $350/tC (US $95 per tonne of carbon dioxide)." See IPCC 2007a, p. 17.

3. The modeling runs assume that emissions reductions occur according to the Kyoto Protocol in 2008–2010. The specific plans analyzed are assumed to begin in the second full model period, 2011–2020.

4. This simplified version was derived in Nordhaus 1991, equation (9). This approximation is just that because the shortcut derivation makes many simplifying assumptions.

Chapter VI
The Economics of Participation

1. Although the DICE-model functional form for abatement costs leads to a particularly neat solution for the costs of nonparticipation, the key assumption is actually the separation into harmonized participating and nonparticipating regions. Even if the functional form were not log-linear, as is assumed and seen in the text, the basic relationship would be similar and would depend on the average degree of convexity in the relevant range if the separation of countries and industries is as assumed.

2. Many disaggregated models have compared the cost of incomplete participation to global trading of the kind summarized here. Estimates are generally in the range of 2.1 to 4.1 times the cost of complete participation, depending upon the model, disaggregation, and time horizon. See Weyant and Hill 1999 for a discussion.

3. This approach was independently and previously suggested to me by Robert Stavins, and a discussion is contained in Aldy, Barrett, and Stavins 2003. The Bush proposal is presented in White House 2007. The Bush initiative is described as follows: "The proposal seeks to bring together the world's top greenhouse gas emitters and energy consumers. In creating a new framework, the major emitters will work together to develop a long-term global goal to reduce greenhouse gases. Each country will work to achieve this emissions goal by establishing its own ambitious mid-term national targets and programs, based on national circumstances. They will ensure advancement towards the global goal with a review process that assesses each country's performances." This was described by Jim Connaughton, chairman of the Council on Environmental Quality, as "a long-term aspirational goal."

Chapter VII
Dealing with Uncertainty in Climate-Change Policy

1. This result about the relationship between the expected-value and the best-guess results differs from many earlier studies. The major reason is that a nonlinearity is found in similar studies but not in this book because earlier studies often include uncertainty about interest rates or the rate of time preference. In the author's view, these are inappropriate uncertain variables in this context because they are either endogenous (for interest rates) or a taste variable (for time preference) rather than an uncertainty about technology or nature. In the uncertainty runs presented here, there is considerable uncertainty about the long-run real interest rate on goods, reflecting uncertainty about the growth in per capita consumption, so the determinants of the uncertainty about interest rates are already implicitly included. Uncertainty about preferences is a different matter. There is no obvious interpretation of uncertainty about preferences such as the time discount rate, and it is for this reason that uncertainty about preferences is excluded. To include uncertainty about tastes in a decision-theoretic framework would require some kind of metataste that evaluates the different taste outcomes.

2. See Merton 1969.

3. See National Research Council, Committee on Abrupt Climate Change 2002 for a review of the science and the societal implications.

4. IPCC 2007b, p. 752.

5. Ibid., chap. 6.

6. See "Polar Science" 2007 for a review of the major findings. See particularly the review in Shepherd and Wingham 2007.

7. IPCC 2007b, p. 776.

8. Ibid., p. 777.

9. See Tol 2003.

10. See Weitzman 2007a.

11. A skeptical review of Weitzman's results is contained in Nordhaus 2007c.

Chapter VIII
The Many Advantages of Carbon Taxes

This chapter is a revised version of Nordhaus 2007e.

1. This distinction is drastically simplified. For a nuanced discussion that includes variants and hybrids, see Aldy, Barrett, and Stavins 2003 and the many references and proposals therein.

2. See Cooper 1998, Pizer 1998, Victor 2001, and Aldy, Barrett, and Stavins 2003.

3. See McKibbin and Wilcoxen 2002 and Aldy, Barrett, and Stavins 2003.

4. See Pizer 1999, as well as Hoel and Karp 2001.

5. See Goulder, Parry, and Burtraw 1997 and Goulder and Bovenberg 1996.

6. See Sachs and Warner 1995 and Torvik 2002.

7. See the pioneering study on ecological taxes in Weizsäcker and Jesinghaus 1992.

8. From a technical point of view, the hybrid plan sketched here is a special case of a nonlinear environmental tax, in which the tax is a function of economic or environmental variables.

Chapter IX
An Alternative Perspective: The *Stern Review*

This chapter is a revised version of Nordhaus 2007d.

1. The printed version is Stern 2007. Also, see the electronic edition provided in the references at UK Treasury 2006. It is assumed that the printed version is the report of record, and all citations are to the printed version. The printed version contains a "Postscript" that is in part a response to early critics, including a response to the November 17, 2006, draft of this review.

2. Stern 2007, p. xv.

3. This strategy is a hallmark of virtually every study of intertemporal efficiency in climate-change policy. It was one of the major conclusions in a review of integrated assessment models: "Perhaps the most surprising result is the consensus that given calibrated interest rates and low future economic growth, modest controls are generally optimal" (Kelly and Kolstad 1999). This result has been found in all five generations of the Yale/DICE/RICE global-warming models developed over the 1975–2007 period. For an illustration of the ramp, see Figures 5-4 and 5-5.

4. For a recent warning, see Hansen et al. 2006.

5. An early precursor of the *Stern Review* is the study by Cline (1992). Cline's analysis of discounting was virtually identical to that in the *Stern Review*.

6. A large body of commentary on the *Stern Review* has been published. A critical discussion of key assumptions is provided in Tol and Yohe

2006 and Mendelsohn 2006. A particularly useful discussion of discounting issues is contained in Dasgupta 2006. An analysis that focuses on the extreme findings of the *Stern Review* is Seo 2007. A discussion of ethics is in Beckerman and Hepburn 2007. A sensitivity analysis of the ethical parameters with much the same message as this chapter is Mityakov 2007. A wide-ranging attack on various elements is contained in Carter et al. 2006 and Byatt et al. 2006. Insurance issues and discounting are discussed in Gollier 2006 and Weitzman 2007b.

7. UK Treasury 2006.

8. UK Joint Intelligence Committee 2002.

9. Stern 2007, p. 530.

10. Arrow et al. 1996.

11. Many of the issues involved in discounting, particularly relating to climate change, are discussed in the different studies in Portney and Weyant 1999. A useful summary is contained in Arrow et al. 1996. A discussion of the philosophical aspects of Ramsey's approach is contained in Dasgupta 2005.

12. See Ramsey 1928, Koopmans 1965, and Cass 1965. Most advanced textbooks in macroeconomics develop this model in depth.

13. Stern 2007, p. 60.

14. The phrase is due to Sen and Williams 1982, p. 16, in which they describe Government House utilitarianism as "social arrangements under which a utilitarian elite controls a society in which the majority may not itself share those beliefs." Dasgupta (2005) discusses Government House ethics in the context of discounting.

15. Koopmans 1965. Zero discounting leads to deep mathematical problems such as nonconvergence of the objective function and incompleteness of the functional.

16. Many of the concerns in the following paragraphs are discussed in the attacks and defenses of utilitarianism in Sen and Williams 1982.

17. This is the spirit of the study of Phelps and Pollak (1968).

18. The interpretation of the divergence between the rate of return on capital and the risk-free rate raises an issue in this context. If we assume that this gap is determined in markets as a systematic premium on risky assets, then we need to investigate the risk characteristics of investments in climate change. The discussion here assumes that climatic investments share the risk properties of other capital investments. If they were shown to have more or less systematic risk, then the risk premium on climatic investments would need to be appropriately adjusted. This question is addressed in Chapter 7 on the risk properties of high-climate change scenarios.

19. The discussion of the consumption elasticity is contained in the appendix to chapter 2 of the *Stern Review* (Stern 2007). Note as well that since the consumption elasticity is a parameter that reflects social choices about consumption inequality across generations, it cannot automatically be derived from individual preferences or risk aversion.

20. This point was emphasized by Dasgupta (2006).

21. Stern 2007, figure 6.5d, pp. 178 and 177.

22. Ibid., box 6.3, pp. 183–185.

23. A simplified derivation of this result is as follows. For this derivation, assume that the rate of growth of consumption is constant at g, that population is constant, that initial consumption is $C(0)$, and that the Ramsey equation holds with the *Stern Review*'s parameters. In this case, the growth corrected discount rate is $\theta = r - g = 0.001$ per year. The wrinkle assumes that there are damages equal to a constant fraction $\lambda = 0.001$ of consumption starting 200 years in the future. Using linear utility, the present value of the damages from the wrinkle is

$$\int_{200}^{\infty} \lambda C(t)e^{-\theta t}dt = \lambda C(0)e^{-\theta 200}/\theta = \lambda C(0)0.818/.001 = 0.818\, C(0).$$

For linear utility, the wrinkle has a present value of 81.8 percent of one year's current consumption. The number in the text is lower because of the curvature of the utility function.

24. Stern 2007, p. 344 ($85 per ton of carbon dioxide and in 2000 prices).

25. Hope 2006.

26. Mityakov 2007.

Chapter X
Summary and Conclusions

1. IPCC 2007b, p.13.

References

Aldy, Joseph, Scott Barrett, and Robert Stavins. 2003. "Thirteen Plus One: A Comparison of Global Climate Policy Architectures." *Climate Policy* 3: 373–397.

Arrow, K. J., W. Cline, K. G. Maler, M. Munasinghe, R. Squitieri, and J. Stiglitz. 1996. "Intertemporal Equity, Discounting and Economic Efficiency." In *Climate Change 1995—Economic and Social Dimensions of Climate Change*, ed. J. Bruce, H. Lee, and E. Haites. Cambridge: Cambridge University Press, 125–144.

Beckerman, Wilfred, and Cameron Hepburn. 2007. "Ethics of the Discount Rate in the *Stern Review on the Economics of Climate Change*." *World Economics* 8(1): 187–210.

Brooke, Anthony, David Kendrick, Alexander Meeraus, and Ramesh Raman. 2005. *GAMS: A User's Guide*. Washington, DC: GAMS Development Corporation.

Byatt, Ian, Ian Castles, Indur M. Goklany, David Henderson, Nigel Lawson, Ross McKitrick, Julian Morris, Alan Peacock, Colin Robinson, and Robert Skidelsky. 2006. "The *Stern Review*: A Dual Critique: Part II: Economic Aspects." *World Economics* 7(4): 199–232.

Carter, Robert M., C. R. de Freitas, Indur M. Goklany, David Holland, and Richard S. Lindzen. 2006. "The *Stern Review*: A Dual Critique: Part I: The Science." *World Economics* 7(4): 167–198.

Cass, David. 1965. "Optimum Growth in an Aggregative Model of Capital Accumulation." *Review of Economic Studies* 32(3): 233–240.

Cline, William. 1992. *The Economics of Global Warming*. Washington, DC: Institute for International Economics.

Congressional Quarterly. 2007. "Gore's Global Warming Plan Goes Far beyond Anything Capitol Hill Envisions." Downloaded from March 21, 2007, online edition at http://public.cq.com/docs/cqt/news11000000 2475002.html.

Convery, Frank J., and Luke Redmond. 2007. "Market and Price Developments in the European Union Emissions Trading Scheme." *Review of Environmental and Economic Policy* 1: 88–111.

Cooper, Richard. 1998. "Toward a Real Treaty on Global Warming." *Foreign Affairs* 77: 66–79.

Dasgupta, Partha. 2005. "Three Conceptions of Intergenerational Justice." In *Ramsey's Legacy,* ed. H. Lillehammer and D. H. Mellor. Oxford: Clarendon Press, 149–169.

Dasgupta, Partha. 2006. "Comments on the *Stern Review*'s Economics of Climate Change." Cambridge University, November 11 (revised December 12).

Edmonds, Jae. 2007. Personal communication, January 10.

Ellerman, Denny A., and Barbara K. Buchner. 2007. "The European Union Emissions Trading Scheme: Origins, Allocation, and Early Results." *Review of Environmental and Economic Policy* 1: 66–87.

EPA (Environmental Protection Agency). 2006. *Acid Rain Program Allowance Auctions.* http://www.epa.gov/airmarkets/auctions/index.html (accessed November 9, 2006).

European Commission. 2006. "European Union Emission Trading Scheme." http://europa.eu.int/comm/environment/climat/emission.htm (accessed November 9, 2006).

Füssel, H.-M., F. L. Toth, J. G. Van Minnen, and F. Kaspar. 2003. "Climate Impact Response Functions as Impact Tools in the Tolerable Windows Approach." *Climatic Change* 56: 91–117.

Gollier, Christian. 2006. "An Evaluation of Stern's Report on the Economics of Climate Change." IDEI Working Paper no. 464.

Gore, Albert J., Jr. 2007. "Moving beyond Kyoto." *New York Times,* July 1.

Goulder, Lawrence, and A. Lans Bovenberg. 1996. "Optimal Environmental Taxation in the Presence of Other Taxes: General Equilibrium Analyses." *American Economic Review* 86: 985–1000.

Goulder, Lawrence, Ian Parry, and Dallas Burtraw. 1997. "Revenue-Raising vs. Other Approaches to Environmental Protection: The Critical Significance of Pre-existing Tax Distortions." *RAND Journal of Economics* 28: 708–731.

Govindasamy, B., K. Caldeira, and P. B. Duffy. 2003. "Geoengineering Earth's Radiation Balance to Mitigate Climate Change from a Quadrupling of CO_2." *Global and Planetary Change* 37: 157–168.

Hansen, James, Makiko Sato, Reto Ruedy, Ken Lo, David W. Lea, and Martin Medina-Elizade. 2006. "Global Temperature Change." *Proceedings of the National Academy of Sciences (U.S.)* 103: 14288–14293.

Hoel, Michael, and Larry Karp. 2001. "Taxes and Quotas for a Stock Pollutant with Multiplicative Uncertainty." *Journal of Public Economics* 82: 91–114.

Hope, Chris. 2006. "The Marginal Impact of CO_2 from PAGE2002: An Integrated Assessment Model Incorporating the IPCC's Five Reasons for Concern." *Integrated Assessment* 6: 19–56.

IIASA (International Institute of Applied Systems Analysis) World Population Program. 2007. "Probabilistic Projections by 13 World Regions, Forecast Period 2000–2100, 2001 Revision." Available online at http://www.iiasa.ac.at/Research/POP/proj01/.

International Monetary Fund. 2006. *World Economic and Financial Surveys, World Economic Outlook Database.* September 2006 edition. Available online at http://www.imf.org/external/pubs/ft/weo/2006/02/data/index.aspx.

IPCC (Intergovernmental Panel on Climate Change). 1996. *Climate Change 1995—Economic and Social Dimensions of Climate Change.* Ed. J. Bruce, H. Lee, and E. Haites. Cambridge: Cambridge University Press.

IPCC (Intergovernmental Panel on Climate Change). 2000. *Special Report on Emissions Scenarios.* Cambridge: Cambridge University Press.

IPCC (Intergovernmental Panel on Climate Change). 2001. *Climate Change 2001: The Scientific Basis.* Ed. J. T. Houghton, Y. Ding, D. J. Griggs, M. Noguer, P. J. van der Linden, and D. Xiaosu. Contribution of Working Group I to the Third Assessment Report of the Intergovernmental Panel on Climate Change. Cambridge: Cambridge University Press.

IPCC (Intergovernmental Panel on Climate Change). 2005. *IPCC Special Report on Carbon Dioxide Capture and Storage.* Ed. Bert Metz, Ogunlade Davidson, Heleen de Coninck, Manuela Loos, and Leo Meyer. Available online at http://www.ipcc.ch/activity/srccs/index.htm.

IPCC (Intergovernmental Panel on Climate Change). 2007a. "Summary for Policymakers." In *Climate Change 2007: Impacts, Adaptation and Vulnerability.* Ed. Martin Parry, Osvaldo Canziani, Jean Palutikof, Paul van der Linden, and Clair Hanson. Contribution of Working Group II to the Intergovernmental Panel on Climate Change, April. Available online at http://www.ipcc.ch/.

IPCC (Intergovernmental Panel on Climate Change). 2007b. *Climate Change 2007: The Physical Science Basis.* Ed. Bert Metz, Ogunlade Davidson, Peter Bosch, Rutu Dave, and Leo Meyer. Contribution of Working

Group I to the Fourth Assessment Report of the Intergovernmental Panel on Climate Change. Available online at http://ipcc-wg1.ucar.edu/wg1/wg1-report.html.

Keith, David W. 2000. "Geoengineering the Climate: History and Prospect." *Annual Review of Energy and the Environment* 25 (November): 245–284.

Keller, K., M. Hall, S.-R. Kim, D. F. Bradford, and M. Oppenheimer. 2005. "Avoiding Dangerous Anthropogenic Interference with the Climate System." *Climatic Change* 73: 227–238.

Kelly, David L., and Charles D. Kolstad. 1999. "Integrated Assessment Models for Climate Change Control." In *International Yearbook of Environmental and Resource Economics 1999/2000: A Survey of Current Issues*, ed. Henk Folmer and Tom Tietenberg. Cheltenham, UK: Edward Elgar, 171–197.

Klepper, Gernot, and Sonja Peterson. 2005. "Emissions Trading, CDM, JI, and More—The Climate Strategy of the EU." Kiel Working Paper 1238. Kiel, Germany: Institut für Weltwirtschaft.

Koopmans, Tjalling C. 1965. "On the Concept of Optimal Economic Growth." *Academiae Scientiarum Scripta Varia* 28(1): 1–75. Available online at http://cowles.econ.yale.edu/P/au/p_koopmans.htm.

Kruger, Joseph, Wallace E. Oates, and William A. Pizer. 2007. "Decentralization in the EU Emissions Trading Scheme and Lessons for Global Policy." *Review of Environmental and Economic Policy* 1: 112–133.

Lutz, Wolfgang. 2007. Personal communications, May 18 and May 21.

MacCracken, Christopher N., James A. Edmonds, Son H. Kim, and Ronald D. Sands. 1999. "The Economics of the Kyoto Protocol." In *The Costs of the Kyoto Protocol: A Multi-model Evaluation*, ed. John Weyant and Jennifer Hill. *Energy Journal*, special issue: 25–72.

MAGICC (Model for the Assessment of Greenhouse-Gas Induced Climate Change). 2007. Tom Wigley, Sarah Raper, Mike Salmon and Tim Osborn, developers. Available online at http://www.cgd.ucar.edu/cas/wigley/magicc/index.html.

Manne, Alan S., and Richard G. Richels. 1992. *Buying Greenhouse Insurance: The Economic Costs of Carbon Dioxide Emission Limits*. Cambridge, MA: MIT Press.

Manne, Alan S., and Richard Richels. 1999. "The Kyoto Protocol: A Cost-Effective Strategy for Meeting Environmental Objectives?" In *The Costs of the Kyoto Protocol: A Multi-model Evaluation*, ed. John Weyant and Jennifer Hill. *Energy Journal*, special issue: 1–24.

Manne, Alan S., and Richard G. Richels. 2001. "U.S. Rejection of the Kyoto Protocol: The Impact on Compliance Costs and CO_2 Emissions." AEI–Brookings Joint Center Working Paper no. 01-12.

McKibbin, Warwick J., and Peter Wilcoxen. 2002. "The Role of Economics in Climate Change Policy." *Journal of Economic Perspectives* 16: 107–129.

Mendelsohn, Robert O. 2006. "A Critique of the Stern Report." *Regulation* 29(4): 42–46.

Merton, Robert C. 1969. "Lifetime Portfolio Selection under Uncertainty: The Continuous-Time Case." *Review of Economics and Statistics* 51(3): 247–257.

Mityakov, Sergey. 2007. "Small Numbers, Large Meaning: A Sensitivity Analysis of the *Stern Review on Climate Change*." February 2. Unpublished paper.

National Academy of Sciences. Committee on Science, Engineering, and Public Policy. 1992. *Policy Implications of Greenhouse Warming: Mitigation, Adaptation, and the Science Base.* Washington, DC: National Academy Press.

National Research Council. Committee on Abrupt Climate Change. 2002. *Abrupt Climate Change: Inevitable Surprises.* Washington, DC: National Academy Press.

Nordhaus, William D. 1979. *The Efficient Use of Energy Resources.* New Haven, CT: Yale University Press.

Nordhaus, William D. 1991. "To Slow or Not to Slow: The Economics of the Greenhouse Effect." *Economic Journal* 101(407): 920–937.

Nordhaus, William D. 1994. *Managing the Global Commons: The Economics of Climate Change.* Cambridge, MA: MIT Press.

Nordhaus, William D. 2001. "Global Warming Economics." *Science* 294: 1283–1284.

Nordhaus, William D. 2007a. "Accompanying Notes and Documentation on Development of DICE-2007 Model: Notes on DICE-2007.delta.v8 as of June 7, 2007." Yale University, June 7. Available online at http://www.econ.yale.edu/~nordhaus/homepage/DICE2007.htm.

Nordhaus, William D. 2007b. "Alternative Measures of Output in Global Economic-Environmental Models: Purchasing Power Parity or Market Exchange Rates?" *Energy Economics* 29(3): 349–372.

Nordhaus, William D. 2007c. "The Real Meaning of Weitzman's Dismal Theorem." September 3. Available online at http://www.econ.yale.edu/~nordhaus/homepage/recent_stuff.html.

Nordhaus, William D. 2007d. "The *Stern Review* on the Economics of Climate Change." *Journal of Economic Literature* 45 (September): 686–702.

Nordhaus, William D. 2007e. "To Tax or Not to Tax: Alternative Approaches to Slowing Global Warming." *Review of Environmental Economics and Policy* 1(1): 26–44.

Nordhaus, William D., and Joseph Boyer. 1999. "Requiem for Kyoto: An Economic Analysis of the Kyoto Protocol." In *The Costs of the Kyoto Protocol: A Multi-model Evaluation,* ed. John Weyant and Jennifer Hill. *Energy Journal,* special issue: 93–130.

Nordhaus, William D., and Joseph Boyer. 2000. *Warming the World: Economic Models of Global Warming.* Cambridge, MA: MIT Press.

Nordhaus, William D., and David Popp. 1997. "What Is the Value of Scientific Knowledge? An Application to Global Warming Using the PRICE Model." *Energy Journal* 18(1): 1–45.

Nordhaus, William D., and Zili Yang. 1996. "A Regional Dynamic General-Equilibrium Model of Alternative Climate-Change Strategies." *American Economic Review* 86: 741–765.

Nordhaus, William D., and Gary Yohe. 1983. "Future Carbon Dioxide Emissions from Fossil Fuels." In National Research Council–National Academy of Sciences, *Changing Climate.* Washington, DC: National Academy Press, 87–153.

Oppenheimer, Michael. 1998. "Global Warming and the Stability of the West Antarctic Ice Sheet." *Nature* 393: 325–332.

Oppenheimer, Michael, and Richard B. Alley. 2004. "The West Antarctic Ice Sheet and Long Term Climate Policy." *Climatic Change* 64: 1–10.

Peck, Stephen C., and Thomas J. Teisberg. 1993. "Global Warming Uncertainties and the Value of Information: An Analysis Using CETA." *Resource and Energy Economics* 15(1): 71–97.

Phelps, E. S., and R. A. Pollak. 1968. "On Second-Best National Saving and Game-Equilibrium Growth." *Review of Economic Studies* 35(2): 185–199.

Pizer, William A. 1998. "Prices vs. Quantities Revisited: The Case of Climate Change." Resources for the Future Discussion Paper 98-02 (revised). Washington, DC.

Pizer, William A. 1999. "Optimal Choice of Climate Change Policy in the Presence of Uncertainty." *Resource and Energy Economics* 21: 255–287.

Point Carbon. 2006. "Historical Prices." http://www.pointcarbon.com (accessed November 9, 2006, by subscription).

"Polar Science." 2007. *Science,* special issue, March 16.

Portney, Paul R., and John P. Weyant, eds. 1999. *Discounting and Intergenerational Equity.* Washington, DC: Resources for the Future.

Ramsey, Frank P. 1928. "A Mathematical Theory of Saving." *Economic Journal* 38(152): 543–559.

Ramsey, Frank P. 1931. *The Foundations of Mathematics.* London: Kegan Paul, Trench, Trubner, and Company.

Ravelle, Roger, and Hans E. Suess. 1957. "Carbon Dioxide Exchange between Atmosphere and Ocean and the Question of an Increase of Atmospheric CO_2 during the Past Decades." *Tellus* 9: 18–27.

Riahi, Keywan, Arnulf Gruebler, and Nebojsa Nakicenovic. 2007. "Scenarios of Long-Term Socio-economic and Environmental Development under Climate Stabilization." *Technological Forecasting and Social Change*, 74(7): 887–935.

Sachs, Jeffrey D., and Andrew M. Warner. 1995. "Economic Reform and the Process of Global Integration." *Brookings Papers on Economic Activity* 1: 1–95.

Savage, L. J. 1954. *The Foundations of Statistics.* New York: Wiley.

Sen, Amartya, and Bernard Williams, eds. 1982. *Utilitarianism and Beyond.* New York: Cambridge University Press.

Seo, S. N. 2007. "Is *Stern Review* on Climate Change Alarmist?" *Energy and Environment* 18(5): 521–532.

Shepherd, Andrew, and Duncan Wingham. 2007. "Recent Sea-Level Contributions of the Antarctic and Greenland Ice Sheets." *Science* 315(5818): 1529–1532.

Stern, Nicholas. 2007. *The Economics of Climate Change: The Stern Review.* Cambridge: Cambridge University Press. Available online at http://www .hm-treasury.gov.uk/independent_reviews/stern_review_economics _climate_change/sternreview_index.cfm.

Teller, E., L. Wood, and R. Hyde. 1997. *Global Warming and Ice Ages: I. Prospects for Physics-Based Modulation of Global Change.* 22nd International Seminar on Planetary Emergencies, Erice (Sicily), Italy, August 20–23. Available online at www.llnl.gov/global-warm/231636.pdf.

Tol, R. S. J. 2003. "Is the Uncertainty about Climate Change Too Large for Expected Cost–Benefit Analysis?" *Climatic Change* 56(3): 265–289.

Tol, Richard S. J., and Gary W. Yohe. 2006. "A Review of the *Stern Review*." *World Economics* 7(4): 233–250.

Torvik, Ragnar. 2002. "Natural Resources, Rent Seeking and Welfare." *Journal of Development Economics* 67: 455–470.

UK Joint Intelligence Committee. 2002. *Iraq's Weapons of Mass Destruction: The Assessment of the British Government.* September (unclassified).

UK Treasury. 2006. *Stern Review on the Economics of Climate Change.* http://www.hm-treasury.gov.uk/independent_reviews/stern_review _economics_climate_change/sternreview_index.cfm (accessed November 1, 2006).

United Nations. 2007. UNFCCC (United Nations Framework Convention on Climate Change). Available at http://unfccc.int/2860.php.

United Nations. Department of Economic and Social Affairs, Population Division. 2004. *World Population to 2300*. ST/ESA/SER.A/236. New York: United Nations.

Victor, David. 2001. *The Collapse of the Kyoto Protocol and the Struggle to Slow Global Warming*. Princeton, NJ: Princeton University Press.

Webster, Mort D. 2002. "The Curious Role of Learning: Should We Wait for More Data?" *Energy Journal* 23(2): 97–119.

Weitzman, Martin. 1974. "Prices versus Quantities." *Review of Economic Studies* 41: 477–491.

Weitzman, Martin. 2007a. "On Modeling and Interpreting the Economics of Catastrophic Climate Change." October 29. Unpublished paper.

Weitzman, Martin. 2007b. "The *Stern Review* on the Economics of Climate Change." *Journal of Economic Literature*, 45 (September): 703–724.

Weizsäcker, Ernest U. von, and Jochen Jesinghaus. 1992. *Ecological Tax Reform: A Policy Proposal for Sustainable Development*. London: Zed Books.

Weyant, John, and Jennifer Hill, eds. 1999. "The Costs of the Kyoto Protocol: A Multi-model Evaluation." *Energy Journal*, special issue.

White House. 2007. "Fact Sheet: A New International Climate Change Framework." Available at http://www.whitehouse.gov/news/releases/2007/05/20070531-13.html.

Wigley, T. M. L., R. Richels, and J. A. Edmonds. 1996. "Economic and Environmental Choices in the Stabilization of Atmospheric CO_2 Concentrations." *Nature* 379: 240–243.

Index

discount rate and, 59–62; *Stern
Review* and, 169–79, *189*
Regional aggregation: as conten-
tious issue, 63–64; DICE-2007
revisions, 47–48, *48, 49*
Rents, quantitative versus price
approaches and, 159
"Resource curse," 159
Revenue transfers, 201–2
RICE model (Regional Integrated
model of Climate and the
Economy), 33, 64; carbon tax
assumptions and DICE, 112,
113, 114–15
Risk premium, high-climate-
change outcomes and, 137–42,
139
Russia, 157, 159

Savage, L. J., 124
Social cost of carbon, 11–12; DICE
conclusions, 196–97; DICE run
of alternative policies, *82–83*,
91, *92–94*, 95; *Stern Review* and,
186; uncertainty and, 129, *130*,
132, 134, 136–37, *136*
Social welfare function, 60–62;
DICE model, 33–35, 39–40, 50;
Stern Review and, 171–79
*Special Report on Emissions Sce-
narios* (IPCC), 47–48, *49*, 53
Stern, Nick, 168
Stern Review: carbon price, *93–94*;
CO_2 emissions and concentrations, 99, *101–3*, 103, *104*;
DICE conclusions and, 197–98,
200–201; DICE run summary,
82–83; emissions-control rates,
95, *97–98*, 99; full name of, 165;
global temperature change, 105,

106–7, 108; incremental costs,
86–90, *87, 89–90*; methodology
and conclusions of, 165–69,
190–91; as policy alternative, *67*,
75–76; relative to baseline
policy, *85*
Stern Review, discount rate and,
168–91; inefficiency of, 179–81,
190–91; optimal economic
growth and social welfare
function, 171–79; strategies
contrasted to DICE, 184–90,
188, 189; zero-discounting and,
76, 181–86
Sulfur-dioxide trading program, of
EPA, 153–55, *155*

Temperature constraints. *See*
Climate constraint policy, with
temperature constraints
Time discount rate, 60–62,
170–71; *Stern Review* and, 76,
171–79, 181–88
Tol, Richard, 146
Tradable allowances, carbon taxes
and, 153–56

Uncertainty, 123–47, 193, 215n1
(chap. 7); abrupt and catastrophic climate change and,
143–47; DICE model appli-
cations, 134–37; DICE model
equations and, 62–63; different
variables and, 129–34; expected
utility model and, 27–28; price
versus quantitative approaches
and, 152–53; purpose of analysis
of, 123–25; risk premium and
high-climate-change out-
comes, 137–42, 201; technical